A Writer's Resource Guide from Creative Connex

# The Spiritual Life Writing Workbook

From Concept to Bookshelf

Susan Scott with Lana Cullis and Sharon S. Hines

The Spiritual Life Writing Workbook: From Concept to Bookshelf

by Susan Scott with Lana Cullis and Sharon S. Hines

spirituallifewriters.com

Copyright © 2025 The Contributors

Book Cover: Katherine Nutt
Graphic Elements: Katherine Nutt
Lana Cullis Photo: Shannon Grantham
Sharon S. Hines Photo: Rick Schwartz
Susan Scott Photo: Ron Grimes

ISBN: 9 781738 225729

First Edition

All rights reserved. No portion of this book may be reproduced, distributed, transmitted, downloaded or changed in any form or by any means whether electronic or mechanical, including photocopying, recording, or by any information storage and retrieval system, without express written permission from the Authors.

For bulk or group purchases, please email us at info@creativeconnex.ca.

# Table of Contents

Introduction ................................................................................................. 1
    So, What Is Spiritual Life Writing? ................................................... 1
    How to Use This Workbook ............................................................... 3
    Our Expertise ....................................................................................... 4
    Themes and Trends ............................................................................. 5

Chapter 1 LET'S GET STARTED ................................................................ 9
    If You're Totally New to Writing ..................................................... 11
        Choosing a Topic ........................................................................ 11
        Spewing ....................................................................................... 13
        Drawing a Mind Map ................................................................. 16
    Planning the Journey ........................................................................ 18
        Clarifying Your Why .................................................................. 18
        Choosing a Genre ....................................................................... 19
        Finding Conversation Partners ................................................... 20
        Picturing the Audience ............................................................... 22
    Gathering What You Already Have ................................................. 23
    Grounding Your Research ................................................................ 25
        Finding the Right Experts .......................................................... 25
        Beginning Your Research ........................................................... 25

Chapter 2 MAPPING THE JOURNEY ...................................................... 29
    Being Realistic about Your Commitment ........................................ 31
    Mapping Your Storyline ................................................................... 34
    Generating That Outline ................................................................... 39
        Assessing Your Writing Style ..................................................... 39

Chapter 3 LET'S GET WRITING ............................................................... 47
    The Drafting Process ........................................................................ 49
        Establishing Your Order of Writing ........................................... 50

- Using Technology to Help .................................................................................................. 52
  - Writing with Chronic Conditions ................................................................................. 53
  - Lana's Experience ........................................................................................................ 54
- World-building .................................................................................................................. 59
  - Susan's World-building Sample and Reflection ........................................................... 63
- Exploring Your Spiritual Context ..................................................................................... 65
  - Writing into the Sacred ................................................................................................ 68
- Waystations, Vistas, and Pitfalls ....................................................................................... 73
  - Learning and Shoring Up Support ............................................................................... 73
  - Vocabulary and Values ................................................................................................. 75
  - Do No Harm ................................................................................................................. 75

## Chapter 4 EDITING and POLISHING .................................................................................. 79

- Editors and Kinds of Editing ............................................................................................. 81
  - Working with Editors ................................................................................................... 81
  - Kinds of Editing ........................................................................................................... 82
- Self-Editing and Revising .................................................................................................. 84
  - The Power of Revising and Self-Editing ..................................................................... 84
  - Revising and Self-editing Methods .............................................................................. 85
  - How Do Revising and Self-editing Relate to Spirituality? .......................................... 86
  - Incorporating Ritual into Your Practice ....................................................................... 89
- Getting Permissions ........................................................................................................... 90
  - Copyright and Quoting ................................................................................................. 91
  - Identifiers: What's in a Name? ..................................................................................... 91

## Chapter 5 PUBLISHING and PROMOTION ........................................................................ 97

- Looking at Options ............................................................................................................ 99
  - Assessing Author Platform ......................................................................................... 100
  - Choosing Traditional, Indie, or Hybrid Publishing .................................................... 101
  - Connecting to Community in Person ......................................................................... 103
- Establishing Your Online Presence .................................................................................. 105
  - Offering an Online Newsletter ................................................................................... 105
  - Building an Author Website ....................................................................................... 107

- Choosing a Domain Name .................................................................................. 109
- Growing Your Online Presence ............................................................................ 110
  - Enhancing Visibility with Social Media .......................................................... 110
  - Maximizing Online Effectiveness .................................................................. 110
  - Leveraging Online Communities .................................................................. 111

## Chapter 6 REFLECTING, CELEBRATING, and BEYOND ............................... 113
- Reflecting on the Process .................................................................................... 115
- Celebrating Your Achievements .......................................................................... 117
- Continuing the Creative Journey ......................................................................... 120

## Chapter 7 BEHIND-THE-SCENES WITH AUTHORS ...................................... 123
- A Peek Behind the Curtain .................................................................................. 125
  - The Truth About Writing by Sharon S. Hines ................................................ 125
  - Submitting to Story by Lana Cullis ................................................................ 129
- Soul Work ............................................................................................................ 133
  - Exploring New Directions by Dora Dueck .................................................... 133
  - Examining Time by Hollay Ghadery ............................................................. 134
  - Reconnecting with Nature by Sheniz Janmohamed .................................... 134
  - Finding Grace & Grounding by Pam Johnson .............................................. 134
  - Speaking Truth to Power by Jónína Kirton ................................................... 135
  - Identifying our Teachers by Betsy Warland .................................................. 136
- Writing as Healing ............................................................................................... 136
  - The Good News by Vickie MacArthur ........................................................... 137
- Writing as Witness .............................................................................................. 138
  - Pots & Pans by Adele Dobkowski ................................................................. 139
  - The Chamber of Yearning by Kitty Hoffman ................................................. 140
- Writing as Invitation ............................................................................................. 141
  - Open to Others by Linda Trinh and Lori Sebastianutti ................................. 142
- Writing and Resistance ....................................................................................... 145
  - Tips for Persisting as a Writer by Meharoona Ghani .................................... 145
- Writing and Service ............................................................................................. 146
  - A New Way Of Publishing by Andi Cumbo & Caroline Topperman ............. 146

| | |
|---|---|
| Chapter 8 ENDNOTES | 149 |
| Resources | 151 |
| Acknowledgements | 152 |
| Meet the Authors | 153 |
| Let's Connect | 154 |
| Chapter 9 PROGRESS TRACKER | 155 |

# Introduction

*Be a lamp, be a ladder, be a lifeboat.*
— Rumi

Do you have a book in you? Do you feel called to write one? Are people asking you to please write that book they've all been waiting for? Maybe you're already published and are ready to take another plunge. Regardless of where you find yourself, now is the time to line up the support you'll need for the remarkable journey ahead.

*The Spiritual Life Writing Workbook: From Concept to Bookshelf* is designed to be that go-to, hands-on guide for adventuring to authorhood and beyond.

If you're a faithful journal-keeper, you already know the perks of committing to a writing practice. Authoring a book is more demanding, especially given the fleeting nature of inspiration and the stamina it takes to finish a solitary project. Imagine capturing that elusive spark, winsome turn of phrase, arresting image, blazing list of questions, or list of doubts at a moment's notice, in the very workbook that offers you clear-eyed advice and stair-stepped guidance. Here, you have space to expand your ideas while you stay oriented to what every author faces: envisioning, planning, researching and writing (and re-writing!), then working with editors and publishers before finally stepping into the marketplace — and into the sun.

We understand what it takes to navigate that territory, and why some would-be authors fall short of their goals. Projects get abandoned. Writers lose confidence, perspective. Some lose heart. To see a book project to completion, you need to recognize paths from pitfalls and know when to tack in one direction and when to double back.

That's why we have created worksheets for each chapter with specific prompts, followed by space for you to experiment and draft your own solutions. A little timely problem-solving can prevent a lot of heartache down the road. By using these pragmatic, friendly worksheets — and your progress tracker — you can review your writing strategies and gain perspective on your choices. Let us help you stay on track, following the heartbeat of your story.

## So, What Is Spiritual Life Writing?

Life writing is an umbrella term for personal accounts of human experience. It's that simple. Think journals, diaries, confessions, letters, autobiographies, personal essays, memoirs, biographies, ethnographies, or profiles. Spiritual life writing (SLW) refers to personal accounts of whatever the author deems spiritual, sacred, faith-based, or religious. So, when you try to wrap your head around the notion of spiritual life writing, think broadly.

Heather Walton's *Not Eden: Spiritual Life Writing for this World* argues for the need to think way outside the box, well beyond the notion that the only SLW worth its salt is theological reflection. We agree. Life writing about the sacred goes well beyond belief to touch on every aspect of human experience. Psychology. Health. Sexuality. Education. Vocation. Social status. Food and folkways. And, of course, family. So much is bound up with notions of what's sacred, beyond plumbing mystery, sensing the presence of something numinous or divine, discerning the guidance of a higher power, or receiving ancestral wisdom.

Spiritual life writing comes in many forms and in many voices. We're here to celebrate all expressions.

Take, for instance, the 4th Century classic, *Confessions*, by Augustine, Bishop of Hippo — a volume still in print, still seen as the cornerstone of autobiography and spiritual autobiography in the western literary canon. (You knew that, right? Okay, maybe not.) Or maybe a college student has given you *Meditations*, by the 2nd Century emperor and Stoic philosopher, Marcus Aurelius, whose assertion that "everything is connected, and the web is holy" is still echoed by mystics, pantheists, and Wiccans.

Now, consider a contemporary memoir by a Canadian music icon. At first glance, Bruce Cockburn's *Rumours of Glory* might seem a far cry from a philosopher's musings or the North African bishop's magnum opus. Yet the singer-songwriter wrestles with many of the same themes, including sexuality, the nature of divinity, and what it means to live a purpose-driven life. For obvious reasons, Cockburn's book is marketed as a music memoir. But make no mistake: it is spiritual life writing hiding in plain sight.

The rub is in the labeling.

There's an assumption that the steep decline in religious affiliation in western countries corresponds to a drop in consumer interest (that is, sales). That seems logical, doesn't it? And yet, we're seeing just the opposite. More than ever, people want to express themselves authentically, to speak openly and freely about all aspects of their lives, the sacred and profane included.

And with declining participation in institutional religion alongside the surge in self-described seeking, it's more important than ever that we strive to understand one another's histories, needs, and interests. Historically, faith has been a common denominator in many cultures. Pluralistic societies simply can't afford to sideline faith as a key marker of ethics, values, and meaning.

So, where do you fit into all of this?

We hope you'll think about all the books that have awakened you or spoken to your spirit. Could it be Maya Angelou's *I Know Why the Caged Bird Sings*, James Baldwin's *Notes of a Native Son*, Richard Wagamese's *One Native Life*, Joy Harjo's *Crazy Brave*, Maxine Hong Kingston's

*Warrior Woman*? Did *Unorthodox* by Debra Feldman, or Tara Westover's *Educated*, surprise you?

Of course, what counts as spiritually significant depends on the author and their reader. Naturalist Sharman Apt Russell authored several award-winning works before sharing her worldview in *Standing in the Light: My Life as a Pantheist*, whereas naturalist Terry Tempest Williams made her mark with her searing debut memoir from the Mormon heartland, *Refuge: An Unnatural History of Family and Place*.

Even a passing interest in these titles is a testament to the enduring power of deeply personal works that open up to bigger questions.

Now, where would you place yourself? Wherever it is, may you find yourself in a bold lineage, or a place you can return to for grounding and wisdom. May you converse freely with other authors, living and dead. May you close your eyes and see your book in some magnificent library, shimmering alongside self-published volumes, the latest best-sellers, and classics that have stood the test of time. Whether you're tackling a memoir, drafting a slim volume of poems, collecting personal essays, spinning beautiful tales for children, or inventing a compelling YA series, we are here to help you realize the story that is yours to tell.

## How to Use This Workbook

So, let's say you're committed. Just one thing is holding you back. Fear. A certain sinking feeling. You are not alone. Any writing that touches on faith and family, for instance, is a high-stakes venture that begs the question: why not just let skeletons languish in the closet? You may be wondering why to put yourself through this I-need-to-write-a-book business. Is it this hard for everyone? After all, your boss didn't seem to go through a lot of machinations, penning his golf memoir, and your aunt's quirky children's book didn't raise tricky moral questions, did it?

Your ambivalence is valid. In fact, it's a good sign. Certain moral and ethical considerations come with spiritual life writing. The more you anticipate those, the better the chances that you'll work through them — and maybe help your future readers do so, too.

Still, it's a lot to face head on. The good news is that you have this workbook.

Chapters 1 and 2 offer an on-ramp to help you gear up for the hard work of actually digging into your project. By Chapter 3, you'll soar with "World-building" and "Exploring Your Spiritual Context." By the time you work through "Waystations, Vistas, and Pitfalls," you will be able to confront the very fears that haunt you now. Chapters 4 and 5 provide a gently sloping off-ramp while you revise your manuscript and plan your outreach strategy. Chapters 6 and 7 offer some surprises that we hope leave you renewed, refreshed, and energized.

Meanwhile, at every step of the way, we encourage you to use all the resources at your disposal, and to mix and match to fit your needs. Just remember, you can have confidence that this guide offers something distinctive — the kind of hard-won insight that comes with having learned a whole lot from our own mistakes.

## Our Expertise

The team behind this workbook is practiced in guiding people of all stripes and persuasions, in all walks of life. We — Susan, Lana, and Sharon — specialize in helping people to become better storytellers. Specifically, we help people find a language for expressing their relationship to a higher power, spirit, faith, wisdom-keeping traditions, or religion. Whether your sacred community or spiritual practice is chosen or inherited, celebrated or questioned, or simply examined in the rearview mirror, we are here to help you claim that space.

Together with the innovative team at Creative Connex, we've produced this user-friendly workbook to tote anywhere and pull out anytime you feel the urge to jot, query, doodle, dream, map, organize, disrupt, or simply reflect on the creative process behind your book-creation quest. So, line up your favorite writing instruments, and prepare for a life-changing adventure. We hope that, over time, you'll discover what we have — that answering the call to write is a call to build community and to light the way for others.

Here's a bit about our backgrounds, so you know where we're coming from and why we want you to succeed.

### Spiritual memoir, autobiography, and biography

*I fell hard for powerful stories as a child, listening to the "old people" testify at our small rural church — people opening up about their dreams, visions, and healings, the countless small miracles that marked their daily lives. Finally, studying religion and the arts, I realized that storytelling the world over is bedrock to perceptions of the sacred.*

*My work highlights the sacramental role of the imagination and its power to heal across divides. I've had the honor of working across cultures, in interfaith relations, arts collaborations, and literary publishing, calling stories out of people and guiding them into print. My specialty in this workbook is biography (a subset of history), autobiography (a subset of biography), and memoir (a subset of autobiography). My home, though, is that unsung form with ancient roots and enormous reach — spiritual memoir, the genre hiding in plain sight.* — Susan

### Writing for wellness, sacred memoir, and narrative journalism

*I formerly worked within healthcare settings where the medical model dominates, and diverse cultural and religious beliefs mostly go unharnessed. Honoring spirit and faith in the workplace, as either patient or practitioner, is usually frowned upon. However, I have always felt called to listen to how individuals map sacred stories in seemingly unsympathetic environments.*

*Recently, I have become intensely curious about the potential for narrative journalism to recognize sacred truths within factual reporting. So I often include spiritual references in plain*

*language within the arc of my news publications. For a sample, see my CBC First Person essay, "As a caregiver, I was rarely invited to funerals."*

*Writing is particularly powerful when combined with restorative practices, rehabilitation, and healing. When Faith, spirit, and story are intentionally claimed in this manner, the process becomes transformational; I name this Writing into the Sacred.* — Lana

**Spiritual journaling leading to spiritual memoir**

*I didn't set out to be a writer of creative nonfiction. Or a teacher of it. I set out to be an applied mathematician. And then a corporate trainer. And then a small business owner. And all the while, a keeper of diaries and spiritual journals. From high school, the feedback I got most on my science reports was "Clear and concise." I even got that comment from a boss or two. I was a left-brained writer all the way.*

*And then I heard a call to be a writer of story. Of my story. I had to learn a whole new way to express myself. To write in a way that the average person, a non-scientist, would appreciate. Good thing I wrote all those journals. They are my source material now. And my strength as a writing teacher stems from being in the shoes of the average Joe or Jane who has a story to tell but doesn't know where to begin.* — Sharon

# Themes and Trends

Now, let's say you're struggling to imagine your book out in the world, let alone the notion that anyone would read it. Would it help to know what we notice in our grassroots work with writers? With a couple of exceptions, all titles are from notable small presses or self-published by the author. In other words, if these folks can do it, so can you.

**Social and Climate Justice**

- A chance encounter between a clerk (Seth) and a customer (Clarence) in a second-hand furniture store evolved into a rich collaboration that became *North Wind Man*. Co-authored with Seth Ratzlaff, a young Mennonite settler, the biography tells the story of Clarence Cachagee, who surmounted heartbreaking odds to become a community leader and the founder of Crow Shield Lodge, a place for "reconciliation, land-based teaching, and healing."
- Concerning environmental justice, we're seeing beautiful titles that reckon with our responsibility to heal the Earth and to take climate action. Love is a word that's natural in spiritual life writing. Recent poetry collections by Jannie Edwards (*River, River, Slow Dance* and *Learning Their Names: Letters from the Home Place*), Sheniz Janmohamed (*Reminders on the Path*), Jónína Kirton (*Standing in a River of Time*), and Betsy Warland (*Lost Lagoon*) show us why.
- Carolina Echeverria's memoir-in-progress celebrates her groundbreaking artistic collaborations with First Nations, immigrants, and settlers. To learn about her immersive story-collecting practice, follow the @nativeimmigrantdresses documentary on TikTok.

**Legacy**

Some of the most consequential family sagas are colored by faith — but while one author is honoring tradition, another author might be calling out the impact of religion on a complicated family history. Here are empathetic works by authors who either find the support they need in their home tradition — or who find that the path to integrity lies in questioning the forces of convention.

- In Henry Blumberg's *Sean Left Quietly*, a son's suicide takes the author back in time and history, across continents, to where he finally lands in a place of loving determination with his entire family, trying to offer hope to others who are facing irreversible tragedy, either now, or in their family history.
- Eufemia Fantetti's *My Father, Fortune-tellers and Me* is a moving daughter's antidote to the "lifetime of sickness and sadness" that her ill-matched Italian-Catholic immigrant parents endured, battling untreated mental illness.
- Claudia Putnam's firstborn died in infancy. It took her 30 years to explore the astounding meaning — medical and spiritual — of his untimely death, in what became her award-winning, *Double Negative*.
- Tamara Jong's *Worldly Girls* explores the mixed blessings of her Chinese Scottish ancestry and the challenges of growing up a faithful Jehovah's Witness in 1980s Montreal.

**Identity and Belonging**

- *Saga Boy*, Antonio Michael Downing's breakout memoir, captures "the upheaval of cultural dislocation" and the possibility of reinvention suggested by the subtitle: *My Life of Blackness and Becoming*.
- Gloria Fern's *Saved by Love* recalls her struggle as a rural Mennonite mother-of-three, trying to live authentically, then coming out in the 1980s and going on to become the first gay counselor to serve her community.
- One vital role of small presses is introducing new voices that help the public come to terms with controversial topics. In Hollay Ghadery's propulsive memoir, *Fuse*, gender, race, sexuality, and trauma color her depiction of the pressures facing bi-racial women in conforming to social norms and expectations.
- Caroline Topperman's *Your Roots Cast a Shadow: One Family's Search Across History for Belonging* sweeps across 20th Century Europe and beyond with her Polish family of communists, Catholics, and diasporic Jews to answer the question, where is home — and once we land, will we be allowed to rest?
- Linda Trinh's *Seeking Spirit: A Vietnamese (Non)Buddhist Memoir*, debuts in 2025, but you may already know her as the beloved author of the award-winning children's series, The Nguyen Kids, in which she explores faith issues with curiosity, empathy, and care.
- *Works-in-progress*: Montreal writer and rabbi Kitty Hoffman and Southern Ontario writers Lori Sebastianutti (Italian-Catholic) and Laura Sergeant are all building their

literary street cred by releasing essays based on their forthcoming books. Look for these emerging writers in award-winning magazines and journals.

**Mind, Body, Spirit**

- Donna Costa published her mother's draft autobiography under the title, *Transformation*, to suggest what it meant for a 1940s city girl to become a rural newspaper columnist. Donna's own writings explore lasting mother-daughter bonds, and the "voices in her head" that have become her trusted guides.
- *In Two Voices*, by Linda E. Clarke and Michael Cusimano, MD, brings a writer and her neurosurgeon into a revealing conversation about her life-altering surgery in his hands.
- Joy Thierry Llewellyn is a B.C.-based pilgrim-par-excellence whose YA novels introduce young people to the Camino de Santiago, ashrams, and other numinous sites around the globe.
- Vickie MacArthur's *A Lotus on Fire: How a Buddhist Monk Ignited My Heart* is an epistolary (written in letters) memoir and intimate account of grieving and awakening that opens to the power of love beyond boundaries.
- *Works-in-progress*: Penny Allport's uncommon journey to becoming a life cycle celebrant and minister informs the luminous stories within her future memoir, Moving Ceremonies. Poet Meharoona Ghani isn't waiting until her book comes out either. She's taken excerpts from Letters to Rumi to the stage, collaborating with musicians and other artists to bring her hybrid (poetry and prose) epistolary memoir to life.

Here's to you, new author. You can do it!

*Susan, Lana, and Sharon*

# Worksheet

## 0.1: Explore spiritual life writing

Writing is a superhighway for reflection. The more we share our reflections, the better chance we have of understanding one another and building a world that is tolerant and just. To act for the collective good in ways that are grounded, respectful, empathetic, and diverse, we need to center stories. Which is great news, because, really, what's more portable than stories? Folks from five to 95 relish storytelling. That makes spiritual life writing essential to your kit on the quest for self-knowledge and for shoring up community.

Begin by reflecting on spiritual life writing as you know it: the books and authors that are, for you, iconic; the voices you respect; those companions you turn to for inspiration. Think about how those guides might be of help as your project is starting to take shape.

For more specific guidance and prompts, see Chapter 3, "Exploring Your Spiritual Context" and "Waystations, Vistas, and Pitfalls."

**Draft a working definition of spiritual life writing** that fits you. Permit yourself to revise your understanding as your project grows and changes.

# Chapter 1
# LET'S GET STARTED

*The beginning is always today.*
—Mary Shelley

*Fill your paper with the breathings of your heart.*
—William Wordsworth

# If You're Totally New to Writing

This section is for you if you feel that writing a book might be something you might want to try (on your bucket list, perhaps?), but you're unsure what to write, or where to begin. First, the good news: writing happens in stages. Despite what you've seen on TV or in the movies, writers don't just sit down at a keyboard, type in the title of their manuscript, and continue typing until THE END.

The worksheets will help you explore some possible topics. Feel free to repeat the exercises often; they're designed to help you loosen up and explore options. Think of the process as trying on different ideas for size. You don't have to choose between them. You're laying out the possibilities, to contemplate before you choose — or change your mind altogether.

## Choosing a Topic

Philosophers, mystics, and poets say that language for the ineffable is limited. And, well, it is. That can make writing about the sacred intimidating. Yet, here we are, presenting you with this friendly workbook, encouraging you to embrace the challenge of simply writing about your experiences. Just to see what happens.

We believe in this approach because we've seen how transformational it can be. But the key at the beginning is to keep things simple. A good topic for your book could range from one incident you explore in detail to a challenge faced over many years. If you feel strongly that you have a story that needs telling, listen to that instinct. Here are some questions to get started:

- What trial(s) have you overcome that someone else might relate to?
- What life lessons have you learned? Where, or how, did you acquire them?
- What life experiences have you had that you'd like to explore?

This isn't an exhaustive list. It's intended to trigger your memory and get you thinking broadly about how to mine your own life for insights worth sharing. Here's a sample list written by Sharon; use it as a springboard for your worksheet.

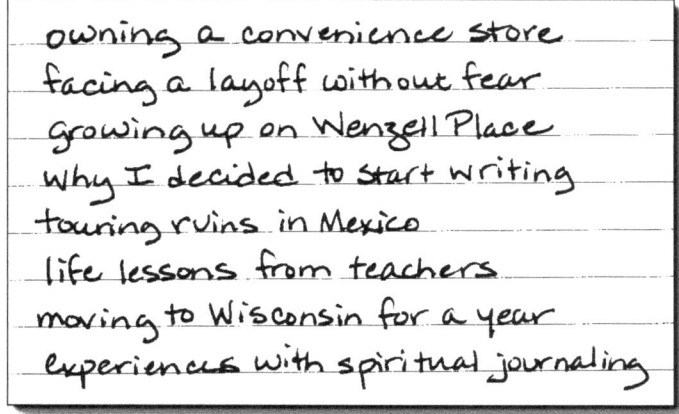

# Worksheet

## 1.1: Choose a topic

**Set a timer** for two minutes. **List as many story topics as possible.**

Mind the timer, so you don't overthink things. Your topics might be compelling, mysterious, or transformative life moments. Or maybe what springs to mind are ordinary things that grounded you when everything (or everyone) around you was chaotic. Some things may have happened over a short period, while others might be multi-year journeys. The point of this exercise is to prime the pump, and simply get ideas flowing.

Move quickly, using short phrases and bullet points, rather than full sentences. You can always come back, to develop into topics.

Now, **review the list.** If you realize that nothing calls to you as a book topic — something you feel you can commit to — do another two minutes. Or take a break to clear your head, then do the exercise again. Don't be surprised if you wake up the next day with more ideas. Write them all here. Let your list blossom over time.

# Spewing

Once you have a potential topic in mind, try spewing. Spewing is a way to get ideas related to that topic out of your brain and onto the page as quickly as possible. The goal is to write ideas down without stopping to analyze or edit them in any way. In short, let's bypass those inner gatekeepers! For now, you want a list of key points, not the whole story. Here are some suggestions:

- Bullet points are better than complete sentences.
- Order doesn't matter.
- Grammar and spelling do not matter either (yet).

Let's gear up for the worksheet. Prepare to write without stopping. Keep going for the entire ten minutes even if you think you're done. If you get stuck, just write "I don't know what to write." This permission-giving, free-flow writing encourages your subconscious to step in and fill the void.

In the example shown, Sharon created a list of lessons by thinking of the people in her life. Your list might take another form, such as events on a timeline, a series of experiences, or a list of travel destinations.

```
Life Lessons

dad - God will take care
    - being careful with things
mom - writing advice
    - being a momma bear
Grandma G - bloom where you are planted
Grandma C - working from home
Auntie A - letting your light shine
Auntie M - how to change a diaper
Grandpa C - the cost of not forgiving
Uncle W - having a back-up plan
Aunt J - life after divorce
Cousin L - being a mom
Uncle P - taking care of family
Mrs. R - being a spiritual leader
Mr. R - paying it forward
Grandpa H - using everything you've got
Uncle WC - lightening the mood
Cousin D - choosing who to support
Cousin TS - being a dad
Cousin TS 2 - knowing yourself
Mrs. M - 3 pairs of underwear
```

Next, go back through your spewed bullet points and see if you can do a bit of preliminary organizing.

- If your list is time-dependent, circle the turning points or key experiences.
- Otherwise, identify three to six categories (for example, themes or other commonalities), and indicate the category for each item on your list. Some people like to have roughly the same number of items in each category. Then again, having several items suggests there is more material to explore. You may need to make a second pass until the list is balanced to your satisfaction.

In the example, Sharon started with four categories. She broke the largest category (family) into two and eliminated an item.

Life Lessons

- G  dad - God will take care
- S  - being careful with things
- C  mom - writing advice
- FP  - being a momma bear
- G  Grandma G - bloom where you are planted
- C  Grandma L - working from home
- C  Auntie A - letting your light shine
- FP  Auntie M - how to change a diaper
- FR  Grandpa C - the cost of not forgiving
- C  Uncle W - having a back-up plan
- F  ×Aunt J - life after divorce
- FP  Cousin L - being a mom
- FR  Uncle P - taking care of family
- G  Mrs. R - being a spiritual leader
- S  Mr. R - paying it forward
- S  Grandpa H - using everything you've got
- FR  Uncle WC - lightening the mood
- FR  Cousin D - choosing who to support
- FP  Cousin TS - being a dad (balance)
- G  Cousin TS 2 - knowing yourself
- S  Mrs. M - 3 pairs of underwear

F = family   9   { P = parenting
S = stewardship   4   { R = relationships
G = God/spirituality   4
C = career   4

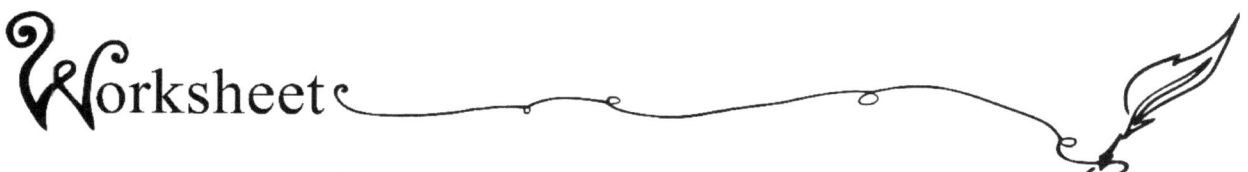

## 1.2: Spew your thoughts

**Set a timer** for ten minutes. **Explore all you can about one topic** as a possibility for your book. Write down everything you can think of related to this topic.

**Do some preliminary organizing.** Set a timer for two minutes, then identify turning points or categories.

# Drawing a Mind Map

Drawing a mind map of key points or stories is a way to organize your thoughts visually. Once you create a mind map, it's an easier task to draft a storyline, and eventually, an outline. Here are the basics of mind-map creation.

- Place your topic or theme at the center of the page.
- Arrange group titles around this central idea, corresponding to the turning points, key experiences, or categories identified from the spewing exercise.
- Connect more detailed items from the list to their related group titles.
- Items may be added, dropped, or edited throughout the process.

Here is Sharon's mind map:

## 1.3: Draw your mind map

**Set a timer** for ten minutes. **Write your chosen topic at the cente**r of the page. Now **organize key points**, or categories, around it. Connect other items on your spew list, indicating how they fit into key points/categories. If you get stuck, simply move to another path. Include just enough detail to jog your memory later.

# Planning the Journey

Just having a topic and a mind map is a good start. It suggests you're on your way to developing a plan. Add to this the elements below; if you have a handle on these before you begin writing, you're less likely to worry about bogging down or losing your way.

## Clarifying Your Why

It's important to get clear with yourself why you are writing. What is your motivation? If you have a regular journaling practice, then you have an outlet for exploring that question. Either way, being clear about your *why* for a specific project will help you determine its scope — what you want to include or leave out.

Keeping your *why* in mind will also help you to keep going if you feel you're in danger of running out of steam or encountering roadblocks. These are common when it comes to solitary projects that take stamina, self-confidence, and a serious time commitment.

The good news is that there is a wonderful community element at work when it comes to spiritual life writing. Consider some of the many "whys" other writers have when they start writing:

- To express themselves or deepen their creative outlet.
- To explore writing as a spiritual discipline.
- To investigate, or understand, the meaning of their experiences.
- To find an authentic language for the sacred.
- To re-evaluate long-standing assumptions or interpretations.
- To leave a legacy, share hard-to-voice experiences with others.
- To inspire other people.
- To contribute to spiritual life writing conversations, be a part of something greater than themselves.
- To fulfill the call, or respond to the urge, to write.
- To add to their income.

# Worksheet

## 1.4: Clarify your why

**Explore your reason(s) for writing.** Why do you feel called to your current project? Just listing surface elements might not be the whole story. Try digging deeper by asking "why" again in response to your first answer. Sometimes it takes four or five rounds to get to the root cause. Prepare to be surprised once you do!

## Choosing a Genre

As if the classic genres of nonfiction, fiction, and poetry weren't enough, hybrid works (a mix of genres) are becoming common, especially among memoirists. All these genres are popular with readers, so unless you're wed to one, try experimenting. Be adventuresome. Read widely. Take courses. Slip outside your comfort zone. The earliest stages of a project are open-ended. Take advantage of this period of discovery. You might surprise yourself by finding that the genre chooses you.

# Worksheet

## 1.5: Choose a genre

**Record your thoughts and questions about genre.** Think about which genres appeal to you and why. Which are you willing to research or develop for the sake of your project? Try to take into account why you're writing this particular book. Does the genre you're considering dovetail with your *why*? The more you can align these elements, the more satisfying the writing process can be.

*I heard the call to write a book after twenty years of listening to Spirit and heeding Their guidance. Ten years of experimentation later, I discovered the relatively new genre of spiritual memoir. In that moment, everything just clicked. I now write about my experiences in allowing a Higher Power to have the conn.* — Sharon

## Finding Conversation Partners

By conversation partners, we mean those voices that inspire and challenge you to engage in writing and publishing. Your conversation partners may include friends and confidants, writing partners, book clubs, faith leaders and practitioners, as well as writing teachers or mentors. Books, movies, webinars, and podcasts can all be vehicles for identifying those inspiring voices. And don't forget those dog-eared volumes stacked on your bookshelf. They embody the voices of fail-safe guides — the authors who have gone before you.

## 1.6: Find your conversation partners

**List key works that inform your spiritual life writing journey,** or have played a part in your formation. Try adding to your list of favorites (memoirs, stories, poems, letters, hymns, scripture, and so on). Add works that challenge you or have helped to broaden, or redirect, your thinking. Ideally, you want a range of voices.

**Name the authors you would like to echo.** Say why their writing strikes you as inviting, or as evoking the sacred. Try to be specific. What is it about their writing that gives you access to spiritually centered material?

## Picturing the Audience

It's important to identify your readers while you're still in the planning stages. Begin by thinking of the people you are hoping to attract. Identifying them will be important later, for marketing and promotion — they are the people you hope to meet at bookstores, libraries, book clubs, conferences, festivals, and so forth.

But first, when it comes to writing, it helps if you can write as if you are telling your story to a specific person — ideally, a member of your audience. Picturing that person will help you when you're reaching for the words, stories, and even the kind of tone that your readers will appreciate.

### 1.7: Picture your audience

**Write a quick character sketch** of your ideal (or average) audience member. Including specific details will help you to envision that person as you write. Don't overthink this exercise; just list the characteristics of that special person you imagine would love (or champion or invest in) your work.

Revisit this exercise as often as you like. The more real your audience is to you, the easier it is to connect with your readers as you move through different stages of writing and promotion.

# Gathering What You Already Have

Productivity experts like to say, "work smarter, not harder." So, when it comes to writing about the past, be smart. You've probably been creating source material your entire life, and squirreling it away for future reference. The time has arrived to round up that material. Pull things out of storage and put them all to work.

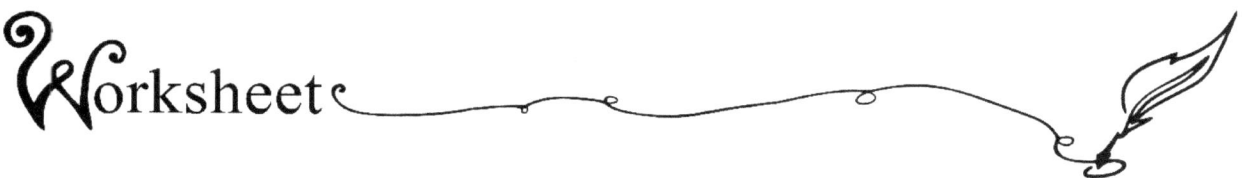

## 1.8: Identify what you already have

**Check off the material you have on hand** that might help with the writing or fact-checking phases of your project. When you're ready to gather the material, look for both paper (or material) and electronic versions. (And, yes, you might need to refile them, or find a new home for these so you can find them easily from now on.)

Make a master list of these resources. Annotate the list, mindful of how each item fits into or touches on your project.

- ☐ letters & emails
- ☐ notebooks & note apps
- ☐ school papers
- ☐ journals & diaries
- ☐ planners & date books
- ☐ scrapbooks
- ☐ the baby book your mom wrote
- ☐ photos & albums
- ☐ cassette recordings
- ☐ home movies & videos
- ☐ speeches & talks
- ☐ sermons & testimonies
- ☐ handwritten index cards
- ☐ legal documents
- ☐ work product
- ☐ newspaper clippings
- ☐ text, voice, or video messages
- ☐ blog articles & web pages
- ☐ comments you left on others' posts
- ☐ anything else you wrote or helped write
- ☐ anything else someone wrote about you

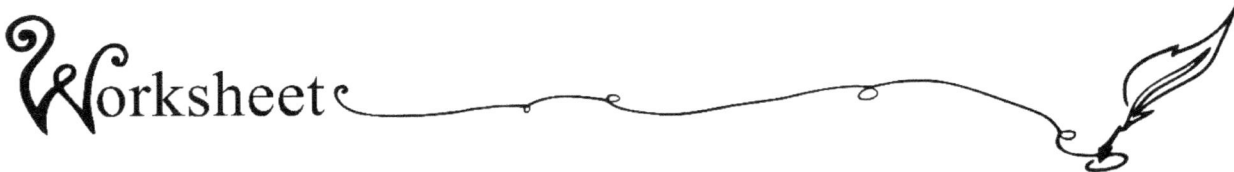

## 1.9: Explore ways to use resources

**Review what you have** and reflect on all the ways to use them. Brainstorm. Be inventive. You can eliminate things as you go, but before you do, try playing with possibilities for combining things, and getting them to "talk" with one another. Meanwhile, here are some nuts-and-bolts questions to consider:

- Do you need to convert hand-written documents or audio recordings to text, so they can be searched easily for the parts to be included in your story? (See Chapter 3, "Using Technology to Help" for tips on media conversion.)

- If you have journals, will you include direct quotes from your entries, or would you be more comfortable summarizing them?

- If you have blog articles or speeches, can you use them as-is, or will you need to tweak them to make that material something you could excerpt?

- Are there photos that are critical to the telling of your story? Could you incorporate those into the book, or are they better used as writing prompts to help you create scenes, or describe your characters in detail?

- Look at the next section, "Grounding Your Research," for ways to use analytical resources and expertise. Ideally, you will build on those in combination with the glorious idiosyncrasy of your personal belongings, resources, and mementoes.

# Grounding Your Research

Researching a project might seem daunting, but the research phase can be liberating, and even a lot of fun. You're starting in one place and landing in another; often it's the discovery phase that points you in the right direction. That "aha" sense that you're onto something can boost your risk tolerance, and trust where the story is leading you, the author. So, embrace the research process. Lining up resources is like organizing files or closets — behind-the-scenes work that frees up mental space. Suddenly, you are seeing patterns. Finally, you know where things belong.

## Finding the Right Experts

Start with the checklist in "Identify what you already have" (Worksheet 1.8). Consider how to mine all that great material. Are there experts or advisors you could talk to? Someone who could deepen your grasp of the subject? Now, look for that expertise in the right places, including archives, reference works, and scholarly conversations.

Archives are often housed in libraries, museums, or cultural centers, making visiting ideal if you can manage that in person. If not, documents and photos that have been digitized are often accessible through an archive's online portal. Either way, if possible, reach out to archivists.

They are trained to help the public interpret a vast range of materials and to see how important papers, official documents, and precious artifacts preserve collective memory and can shed light on the past.

Expert reporting, thoughtful analysis, reference works (bibliographies, dictionaries, encyclopedias, etc.), and sound scholarship are all vital if you hope to present a case or argument, or if you want to reference facts, offer context, add historical or cultural perspective, and so on. You won't go wrong seeking all these out. Quoting reliable leaders in any field shows that you've read widely and have respect for the subject — and those impacted by it.

The trick is to find the right resources for your project. Say you're researching a remote yoga center abroad, or trying to recreate an epiphany you had, walking the Camino. Even memorable experiences fade; in other words, chances are, the details you recall are fuzzy. Simply starting with a map or atlas could keep you from repeating errors or mistaken impressions that may have crept into your notes.

## Beginning Your Research

A little sound research can save you trouble down the line. Here are some things to keep in mind, while you balance the research phase with writing.

- **Frame your research as trying to answer questions.** Something is driving your interest in this project. You're trying to articulate things you care about. You want to figure something out or resolve an issue. Or you simply want to share something meaningful with others. Remember, whatever burning question is driving your research, your book will be the answer to that question.

- **Read widely, and do your own research.** As much as possible, stick with primary sources. Relying on secondary sources (looking at you, Wikipedia) leaves you open to critique; you have no way of knowing if the material is comprehensive or if it has been fact-checked. When in doubt, seek out librarians or professional researchers. It's their job to point authors and researchers in the right direction.

- **Consider the publishers as well as the authors**. When it comes to faith and spirituality — or any topic that is sacred to someone — it's important to understand the mandates of the publishers and presses.

    - Spiritually aligned organizations and faith-based publishers are focused on materials (books, magazines, podcasts, etc.) that resonate with their membership, practitioners, or target audience. Parallax Press, for instance, is the publishing house that presents the works of Thích Nhất Hạnh, so if Zen Buddhists are your audience, you would likely want Parallax titles on your reading list.

    - University presses, on the other hand, are tasked with supporting original research that can be tested, built upon, challenged, and debated. University-based publishers (Oxford University Press, for instance) are often home to reference works, anthologies, and monograms used in higher education and in furthering scholarly research.

- **Consult the latest, or most current, edition**. All authors rethink things. They discover new ideas that challenge their findings or opinions. That means it's important to check the latest editions, then follow up on the impact of that work. Look, for instance, at what the critics say; book reviews are a good place to start. Reading widely will help you fine-tune your ideas so that what you put in print is relevant and timely.

- **Avoid plagiarizing and defaulting to AI.** Imitation may be the sincerest form of flattery, but don't get carried away by the urge to sound like your favorite author. You need to sound like you. Make sure you document your research, so you can find the source you drew on easily and quickly. And, most of all, be sure to write in your own voice. There are plenty of legal and stylistic reasons to do so.

Something else should be said, too. For as valuable as research is, some writers find that phase so enthralling (or anxiety-producing), they're overwhelmed by all the options. Have you ever met someone who boasts a hundred files (or a shoebox filled with index cards) about their characters and plotlines, but who has yet to draft a single chapter? Writer's block can take that form — amassing background material without being able to get to the creation phase of the project.

If you're in danger of being bitten by the never-ending research bug, be gentle with yourself. Sometimes we all need help letting go, to trust that we can return to our sources if, and when we need to.

These worksheets represent a two-step process to keep you moving, so you can stay on track.

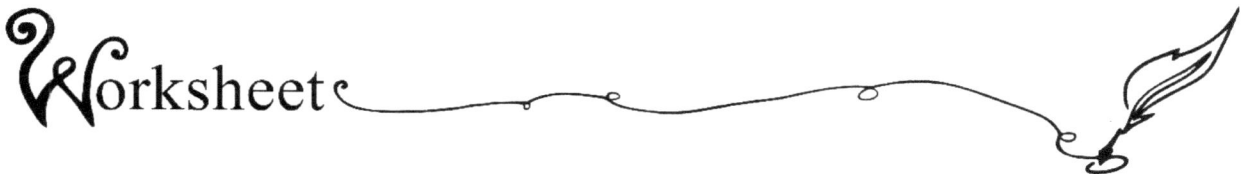

## 1.10: Frame your research questions

**List the key questions you have about your subject** or your project. Try grouping your questions thematically. Refine or regroup as needed. Once you see the big picture emerging, try winnowing the questions, to narrow the scope of your project. A narrow scope keeps things manageable and doable. Remember, you can always expand things (and dust off that shoebox!) later.

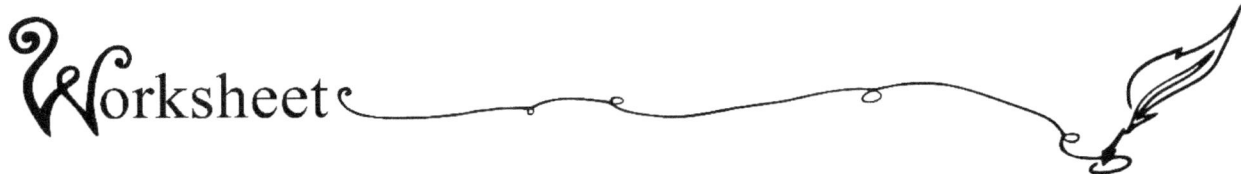

## 1.11: Match resources to questions

**List resources that might help answer your key questions.** Archival materials? Expert analysis? Reporting? Scholarship from different disciplines? Be sure to include all the people and the sites you could visit (online or in-person) to jump-start your research.

Try to think holistically. Naturally, you will be revising and refining your questions as you go. Just remember that whatever or whomever you are drawn to — books, magazines, podcasts, webinars, genealogists, journalists, local history buffs, and so on — researching publishers, parent companies, organizational sponsors, or key supporters will help you identify the kinds of resources that align with your values, needs, and interests.

# Chapter 2
# MAPPING THE JOURNEY

*Do not follow where the path may lead.*
*Go instead where there is no path and leave a trail.*
— Ralph Waldo Emerson

# Being Realistic about Your Commitment

Let's call it human nature: the longer you stretch out the time between your great idea and completing your first draft, the more likely you may never finish. So, before you begin, try to be realistic about what's required to achieve your goal of completing that first draft. Here we're speaking in terms of estimates and calculations, knowing that, for some writers, these terms can be off-putting. Fair enough. Still, it's to your advantage to estimate the time you'll need, and adjust your timelines and expectations as things progress. Here are some tough love questions to consider:

How dogged will you be in finishing this project? How many months do you hope and expect to keep up the effort of staying on course with your writing?

How many hours a day (week, month) can you afford with this one project?

How long is a typical book in your chosen genre? Consider whether a smaller project might be a better alternative to start with.

Remember that allowing time for experimenting, reading and research, and connecting with others, whether that be through courses, mentoring, mastermind groups, or lively conversation, will enrich your entire writing process. You might take a break now and then to gain perspective; a writing retreat or two may even be in order. Do you have experiences or life transitions that change your ability to fulfill your initial plan? Assign realistic numbers to your calculations.

Adopting a holistic approach means taking life changes and life-giving activities into account.

Review your plan periodically, and set aside time to reflect on your calculation process. Writing a book is a big commitment. It takes time, energy, and resources. And not only yours — your writing cycle will also impact other people. Make your wishes known to those most likely to feel some of that impact.

Chances are, those folks will want to be supportive of your work. Regardless, have those conversations, before you over-commit to tasks or roles that may well undermine your creative plans. Ask yourself what, if any, adjustments you could make in your life to gain brief, or extended periods of time to dedicate to finishing that elusive first draft.

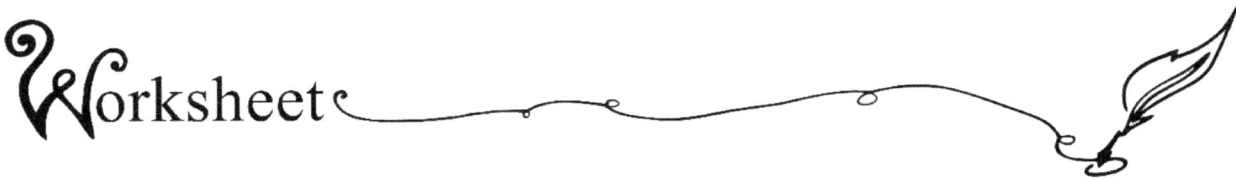

## 2.1: Estimate the required level of effort

Do these calculations so you can see what you're asking of yourself:

Typical length of books in your chosen genre: between _____ and _____ words.

Target length of your book manuscript: _____ words.

Target number of months to finish your first draft: _____ months.

Target number of days per week you plan to write: _____ days per week.

Your writing productivity, on average: _____ words per hour (or day).

Calculate the available days (the number of months divided by workdays per month): _____ days.

Calculate your words per day (length of book divided by number of days): _____ WPD.

Calculate the hours per day (words per day divided by words per hour): _____ hours per day.

Reflect on your calculations. Revise your estimates as needed and revisit these questions periodically to adjust either your schedule or your expectations.

Is this plan **realistic**, given your other commitments?

What targets need to be **adjusted**, if any?

Who will be **impacted** by your writing project, and how will you reach out to them?

What **adjustments** will you make to enable you to finish your manuscript?

What kind of **accountability structure** do you need to help you stay on track? Some people look for an accountability partner; others prefer their own in-house chart, like the Progress Tracker, at the end of the workbook.

# Mapping Your Storyline

Stories, like journeys, turn on action. Story mapping is plotting that course of action. A story map is similar to a travel map. There's the landscape (setting) and key steps (actions) along the way. When writing fiction or a memoir (or biographical work or profile), your focus will be on how your main character changes, say, from ignorance to wisdom, or alienation to community. Mapping allows you to visualize the story arc behind that transformation. Once you see that map, chances are, you'll be able to spot gaps, or the things you would like to fine-tune, from the rising and falling action to the story's overall rhythm, pacing, and so on.

Or, say you're building a collection — pulling together essays, poems, photos, or vignettes. You will want a story arc, so you can turn your book idea and related research into a compelling work that readers want to follow. Mapping lets you gain perspective on your project as a whole, so you can see what, if anything, needs tweaking.

Think of mapping your storyline as planning the itinerary for a trip. Once you have a destination (your main book idea), you explore your travel options (research), then map the steps you'll take along the way.

There are many ways to map or chart a story. We suggest that you go big and go visual. Try using colored markers, and start with a surface you can play on, so you can experiment with options as you go. Try a whiteboard, affix poster board to a blank wall, or draw with erasable markers on a windowpane or patio door.

# Worksheet

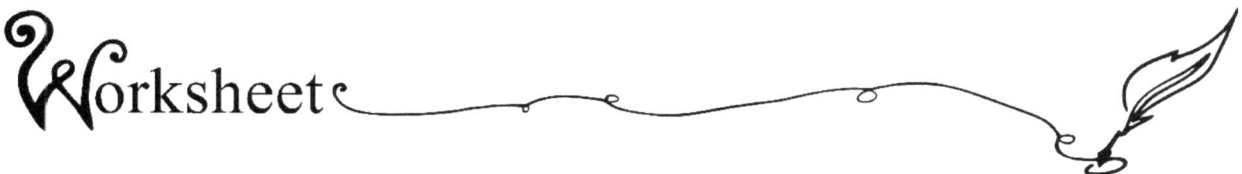

## 2.2: Estimate a timeline

Let's start with time and place. When and where is your story happening? Over what length of time? One location or multiple locations? Are there different locations within the setting? Timelines work well for linear stories — for pieces with a distinct beginning, middle, and end, that unfold chronologically.

Mark and label where and when your story begins and ends. In between, make marks for the main actions and where and when they occur. If there are events that happened in the past, extend your timeline backwards from the beginning to capture backstory or flashbacks. If your story is complex, you may need to draw multiple timelines.

Use the space provided below to **sketch your timeline(s).**

# Worksheet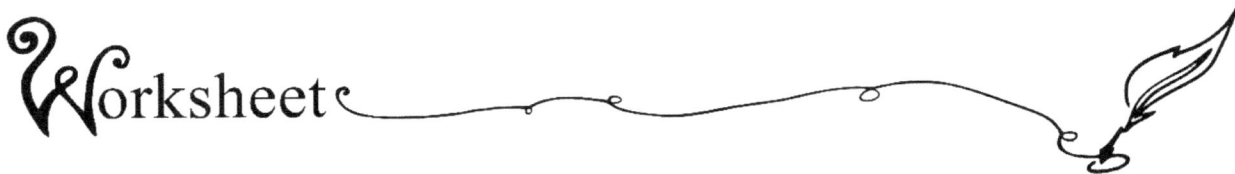

## 2.3: Define a nonlinear story arc

A story (or essay, or collection) might be non-linear, in which case the main elements are organized by theme, rather than a sequence of events. In that case, begin by identifying the main elements of your story on index cards or Post-it notes (there are also app versions of Post-it notes if you prefer to work online). Then play with the order of your elements to establish the arc of your storyline. Try different combinations until a natural or logical order appears. You might be delighted to discover multiple arrangements. If this is the case, take photos of your various layouts and give yourself a couple of days (or more) to mull the options, and discern the direction you want to go.

**Record your elements** in a list below, once you are satisfied with your arrangement. This list will become key for generating an outline, as you will in the next section.

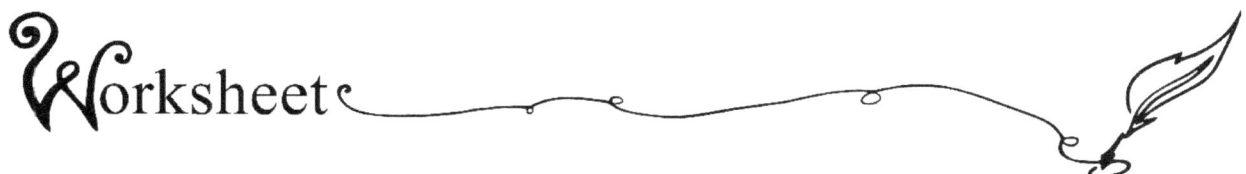

## 2.4: Map a text-based storyline

There is an alternative to visual mapping. It may be that you don't find visual mapmaking especially helpful, or it somehow feels incomplete. If so, a better option might be a text-based technique that involves drafting an opening and closing paragraph to frame your work.

Review your timeline and list from the two previous exercises. Do you sense the essence or shape of your whole story? Take a break and switch activities. Try taking a walk and let your subconscious mull and sort your work. When you return to the page, consider how you will begin your story and what you want your readers to focus on as they move through your work.

What is the narrative question — the problem to be solved, the issue to be resolved, or the transformation being sought — that you want your memoir, essay, or collection to answer?

Now, **write an opening paragraph.** Keep in mind that you will revise it later in your writing process.

Now turn your attention to the end of your book and consider how the narrative question will be resolved. What do you hope the reader will have learned, or come to understand by the time they are finished reading? A conclusion is not solely a re-wording of the opening, and it doesn't simply sum up the entire text; a conclusion marks the major shift that transpired during the journey.

Here's a tip: think of the opening and closing as book-ends that balance and complete one another. A satisfying start to a story has what writers call an "end orientation," where the seeds of the conclusion are embedded in the opening itself.

Take another break, switch activities, or go for another walk and let your subconscious work on this task. When you return to the page, consider how you will end your story and what you want your readers to understand or know as they read the last page of your book.

**Write a closing paragraph.** Remember, you can revise it later in your writing process.

# Generating That Outline

Do you freak out a little when you hear the word outline? You might be tripping over old English class baggage if you worry you will fail at making a "proper" one. Do you worry about feeling hemmed in by an outline before generating your first draft? Those are all legitimate concerns. Even so, many writers advocate working from an outline. Now that you have completed the worksheets up to this point in the chapter, you may have noticed that addressing specific topics within time limits helps to focus your thoughts — and stow away perfectionism. If so, you are in good company. Many writers say that having a structure to guide their production is helpful, providing that structure isn't rigid.

Outlines are detailed maps for your writing project. Think topographical maps vs. hand-sketched traveling directions. Outlines help writers stay on track, plot word counts, set page or chapter content, and ensure the subject of the book is fully addressed. Outlines can be written for smaller chunks of your project, from specific book elements and individual chapters to plot lines and characters. Scrivener is one example of a writing software that provides comprehensive guidance for generating detailed outlines.

## Assessing Your Writing Style

Another way to tackle your relationship with outlines involves determining your writing style. Here, we introduce three distinctive kinds of writers: plotters, pantsers, and planters. (Much has been written about all three.) Plotters are fans of detailed outlines; pantsers are writers who prefer to fly by the seat of their pants; and planters like to do both. If you are an experienced writer, you likely know your type. If you are new to writing, reflect on how you typically approach life. How are you at managing structure? How are you at multitasking, or juggling your job with hobbies, or caring for your home or garden? The answers may suggest your approach to drafting outlines. Here's some insight into how different writers express these styles.

**Meet the Plotter**

*I like to begin writing from some type of basic foundational structure. I create a tentative outline based on a timeline, a mental model, a scripture, or a list of steps to be taken. Then I tweak the outline as I see the need. In writing my first manuscript (an exposition on Christian discipleship), I began with a mental model of the nature of ministry described by Augustine in* The Confessions. *I started with journal entries in my second manuscript (a spiritual memoir). These were very bare-bones descriptions of how God had worked with me over the four months it took to write the first manuscript. As I expanded the journal entries into a full-blown creative memoir, I realized it would help my reader to know about events that had taken place earlier. So, I expanded the story backwards in time, with earlier chapters added. But, except for a few flashbacks in appropriate places, the timeline continued to serve as the basic structure for the manuscript. —* Sharon

**Meet the Pantser**

*I need to experiment before I can even think about an outline. Otherwise, my inner academic will jump up and take over. In my experience, defaulting to a logical structure before finding the heart of a piece can stifle the fullness of expression. By "heart," I mean that each piece has a propulsive energy or distinctive voice; my job is to find and follow it, sense where the voice is leading. It's an intuitive, permissive phase. I'm following my nose — reading widely and making notes, cranking out a lot of nonsense (and some good stuff), and listening for a certain quality of voice (tone, cadence, etc.) that will ultimately guide the project. I court a kind of controlled chaos marked by a lot of generative writing. Once I'm oriented and can stand back to survey the whole, I can distinguish the main route from detours, dead ends, and rabbit holes. At that point, the outline — mostly bullet lists, rich with specificity — often writes itself.* — Susan

**Meet the Plantser**

*I tend to collect loose documents related to my projects in plastic zip folders and start Word docs for online documents and resource links. Then I sketch out my project in a loose and often messy outline (sometimes this will resemble a mind map). I will often use colored pens to map themes. Some things I note to include are submission guidelines, like the topic and word length; sources I know will work well, like books, online resources, or subject interviews; and any sentences or phrases that I have been mulling over pre-writing. At this point, I usually transfer the outline draft to a Word doc and move items under the section headings Intro, Main Points, and Ending. Then I do my first draft and let it sit for a while. Once I have reviewed the draft and made notes, I expand my outline to include new insights and move on to future revisions.* — Lana

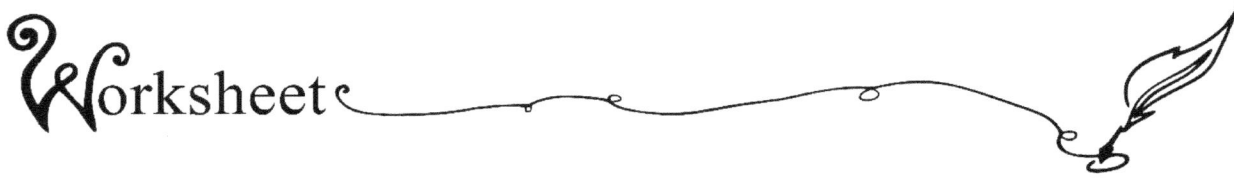

## 2.5: Assess your writing style

Mark on the scale below your current preferred work style.

Pantser ——————————————— Plantser ——————————————— Plotter

If you could change your style, where would you be on the scale?

Pantser ——————————————— Plantser ——————————————— Plotter

Where do you land on the scale concerning making outlines?

Pantser ——————————————— Plantser ——————————————— Plotter

When pitching nonfiction, agents and book publishers typically require an outline and a synopsis of your project. Some writers prefer to draft their manuscript and then create an outline after-the-fact to satisfy these requirements. While this approach is more common than you might think, ask yourself if it's advisable for this specific project. Do you want to put the cart before the horse? Consider how vulnerable you'd be, leaving for a long journey without an idea of your destination, how you will get there, and where you might stay. You can go that route, of course — it will be exciting! But when it comes to writing, wandering has its limitations.

Best-selling author and writing instructor Jane C. Cleland shares highly structured outline forms (with actual book-sample illustrations) in her nonfiction series of craft texts. She writes predominantly fiction (specifically, crime fiction), but her no-nonsense, practical instruction translates well for non-fiction work. Gabrielle Pendergast's *Novel Workbook for Messy Writers* offers a method for organizing writing projects that feels intuitive and favors the pantser's working style (more so than the plotter's). Plotters are the most likely to love author software programs such as Scrivener, which features comprehensive outline designs with pick-and-choose options.

A special nod to writers tempted to skip outlining before writing. Not a problem. Diving in is a valid choice. Frankly, some writers find outlining confining; it triggers their inner perfectionist or critic (see Susan, above). If you're ambivalent about taking the plunge, consider how ordering your work can make a difference. Maybe you're better off amassing free writing, doing character studies, crafting luscious sentences, and then stepping back to see what all you've got. For some writers, allowing for constructive chaos before outlining is the better path, and more rewarding.

In any case, plan to create an outline when the timing is right for you. Only you will know when that is. Here are some red flags to consider: getting stuck in your work, feeling like you are wandering all over the place, or suspecting you are lost; redundancy, as well, can be a sign of lostness. Thankfully, it is always possible to back-track and re-visit drafting an outline for your whole project, or a problematic chapter or section.

So, how comprehensive does an outline need to be? The answer is: as comprehensive as you need it to be; the point is to make the outline work for you. At the very least, a story outline includes your main idea and section-by-section key ideas. You can expand your outline by adding subsections under each major point or idea. Working titles for your chapters can be included too. Outlines often include word counts. Some writers include references to interviews, examples, or research that will inform their manuscript.

A good way to gear up for constructing a book outline is to review your worksheets from "Planning the Journey," "Being Realistic About Your Commitment," and "Mapping Your Storyline." Completing the next two worksheets will help you move from the general (story mapping) to the specific (detailed outlines).

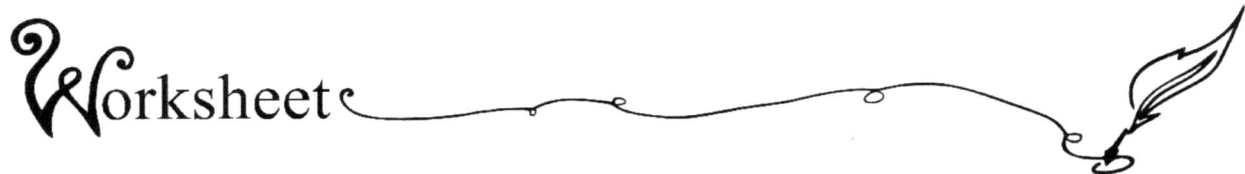

## 2.6: Write your elevator pitch

Imagine you have two minutes to describe the work you are writing to a fellow traveler. That blurb is your elevator pitch — a technique borrowed from employment specialists who guide job seekers and entrepreneurs to express their goals or products more succinctly. It's a compelling scenario, imagining yourself between floors with a maximum of two minutes to hold someone's attention.

Simple right? Not always. You're not alone if you struggle to formulate an elevator pitch for your book. And yet, once completed, that pitch will function like a compass — as an orienting statement that will help you move your entire project forward, including when you approach agents and publishers, and later when you market your book. Let's get you to a place where you can draft that pitch with ease and confidence.

What is the **first thing you would lead with** to hook the listener's attention? Consider using a simple phrase to sum up your story. Additionally, you can use questions, a juicy detail and/or a memorable character to grab attention and pique curiosity.




What are three key bullet points that **expand on your lead?**




What do you want the bystander to remember as you **conclude your pitch?**

Form a paragraph from your responses to **finalize your draft pitch.** A pitch needs to be concise, clear, and compelling as well as relevant, specific, and original. Remember you are pitching your story, not a topic.

Optional steps:

Check out how your pitch lands with others to find out if it's easy to understand, compelling enough to hold someone's attention, or, better still, make them want to buy the book. Start with a safe listener, someone you know to be supportive but who doesn't necessarily know about your project. Then share your pitch with an acquaintance. Notice if your listeners become curious or confused; ask for concrete feedback so you can make meaningful adjustments.

For bonus points, offer your pitch to a stranger. Each round of pitching will help you to refine not only the content but your delivery. Generally, the simpler and more evocative the language, the better for the pitcher and the listener. Ideally, a great pitch rolls right off the tongue.

## 2.7: Create a minimal outline

Use your elevator pitch as a springboard to create an outline by reprinting your pitch in the space below, and separating sentences into introduction, main body, and ending.

On the lines provided between sections, add next-level details for each key point: stories, examples, topics, or concepts. In other words, unpack that lively, cogent pitch and organize its contents. Try to include at least three next-level details per main point (refer to your materials list in "Gathering What You Already Have").

To complete your minimal outline, expand your introduction and ending sections. If you need more space, use additional paper, or draft your minimal outline on your tablet or computer.

Introduction

a.

b.

c.

Main points (you may have more; for instance, an outline section for each anticipated chapter in your book)

1.

a.

b.

c.

2.

a.

b.

c.

3.

a.

b.

c.

Ending

1.

2.

3.

## 2.8: Create a formal outline

Research outline templates and note those that could work for you. Start by finding templates appropriate to the category or genre that fits your needs. There are all kinds of forms to choose from on the Internet that you can download for free. Your local library will also have writing textbooks featuring outlines and how they are used.

Once you have chosen a specific format, move to your computer or tablet to work (if you haven't already). Copy the text from your minimal outline into your chosen template, and proceed to complete your formal outline.

Then take a breath, and celebrate. You are on your way.

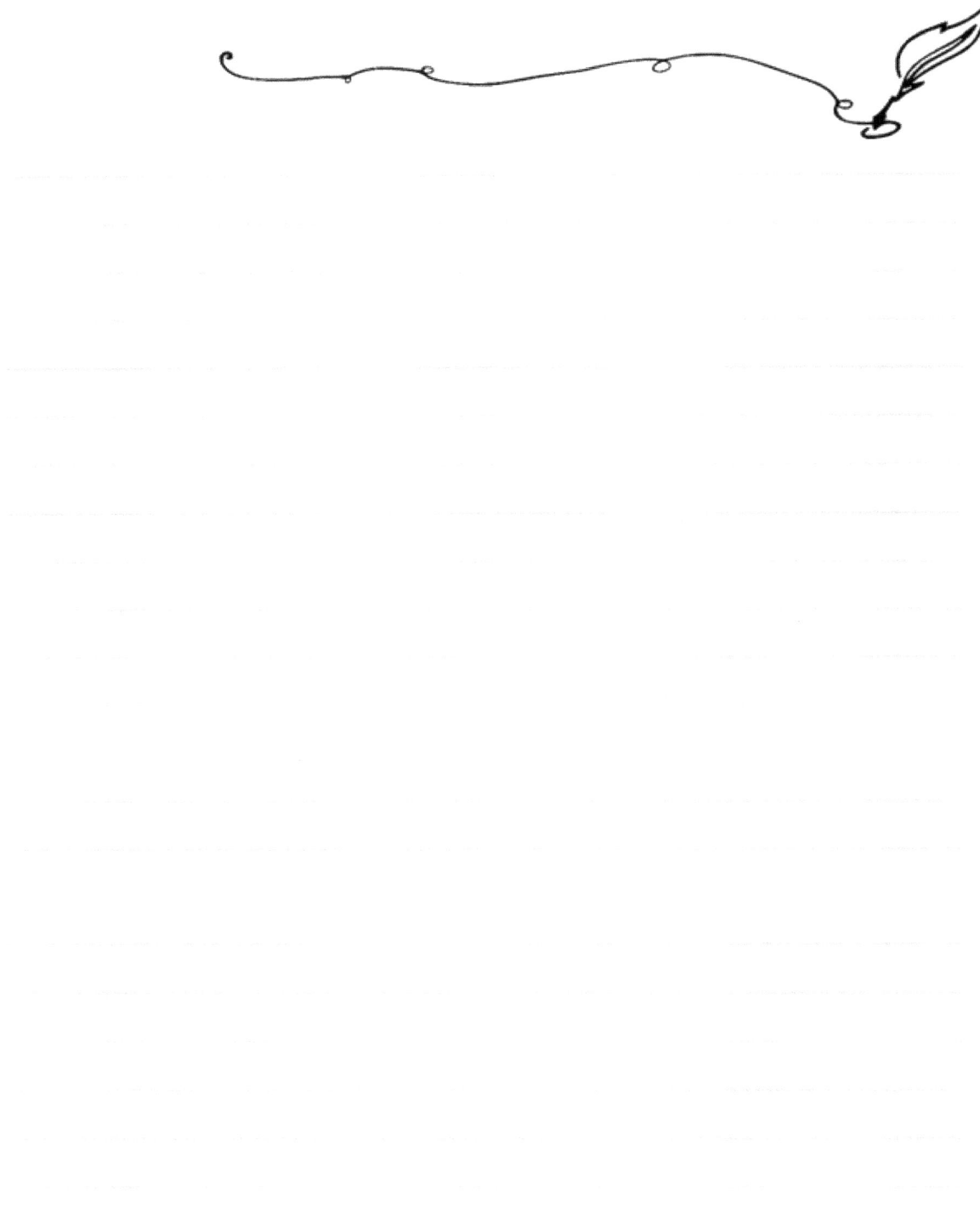

# Chapter 3
# LET'S GET WRITING

*Find out the reason that commands you to write;
see whether it has spread its roots into the very depth of your heart;
confess to yourself you would have to die
if you were forbidden to write.*
— Rainer Maria Rilke

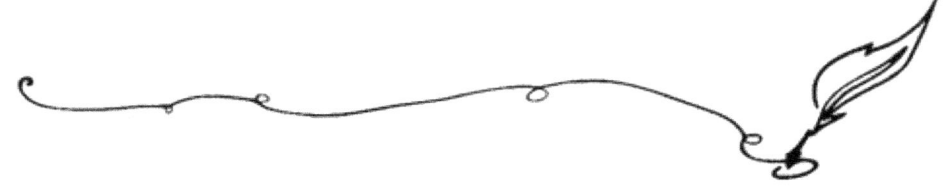

# The Drafting Process

"First draft" can be a rather ill-defined term. Is it the first end-to-end version you've written? Is it the version you hand to someone else for the first time, after you're reasonably happy with it? Is it the version you've arrived at after incorporating feedback from a primary mentor or accountability partner? Maybe we should skip the word "first" altogether.

Writing is a process — putting words on paper, then re-evaluating from every direction, sleeping on it, tweaking here and there, rearranging sections, changing wording, proofreading, cutting out the fluff, tying up loose ends, digging deeper, filling plot holes, asking for feedback, acting on that feedback (or not!), looking at the forest, looking at the trees, in and out, back and forth, until finally, right before publishing, the draft is cast in stone and voila, you have a finished manuscript. That is until the next edition is released.

Let's begin with the process that starts with an outline and ends (eventually) with hitting the PUBLISH key. Author and online writing instructor Jeff Goins uses a sequence of five "drafts" to illustrate these milestones. (Call them by whatever names you like. No one will know.)

Jeff Goins's draft structure:

1. Junk draft: aka vomit, sh**y, or spewing draft — just get it on the page.

2. Structure draft: focus on flow / cohesiveness / consistency — make a go or no-go decision.

3. Rough draft: does it make sense overall? — make it sound good.

4. Surgery draft: slice and dice down to the most essential message — seek criticism and decide ahead of time to apply it (all feedback is a gift).

5. Last draft: make final tweaks — eliminate loose ends.

For our purposes, let's think about your "first draft" as the result of Jeff's first three passes — in other words, the version you're willing to show to someone else. You've gotten it to the point where *you* think the story flows, it makes sense to you, and it's in good enough shape that you're willing to take a leap of faith and invite feedback from others.

Chapter 1 covers basic questions about getting that first spew out of your brain and onto the page. You could just leap ahead (and maybe you already have), but you'll soon run into decisions you will need to make about work processes and wording. One of the first questions is whether or not to begin at the beginning.

## Establishing Your Order of Writing

One of the great things about writing nonfiction is that you already know the ending. (At least, you know where you're headed. That's not always true for fiction writers, especially pantser types.) Knowing the ending already offers you the freedom to compose your first draft in practically any order you like. In other words, you could simply write and assemble sections and subsections as you go.

The question then is, what process works best for you? Are you the kind of writer who functions better if you make a conscious decision early on about what order you want to write the manuscript in? Or do you prefer to explore, and discover the route(s) to your destination? Either way, here are some strategies for getting started:

- Begin with stories you have already written, or have in audio form. Tweak them to suit this new purpose. Then write new material for the remaining sections.

- Decide each day (or week or month) which part of the book is calling to you, and work on that. Once you're happy with a section, or have a draft that you can live with, you can figure out where it fits into the whole.

- Start at the beginning of the book, and follow the outline you created. (Some folks really do that.) Or you might find yourself tweaking the outline to match what you have written, and that's standard practice, too.

These are all valid strategies. You may have yet another one. The best strategy is the one that makes writing the most fun, rewarding, or intrinsically meaningful — pick your adverbs. The more invested you are in staying with your writing, the more likely you are to finish. Be intentional, and reflect on dead ends when you hit them. Don't be afraid to turn around and start over. Remember, in writing, nothing is wasted. You can always re-engage with a piece and rework it until it finds a home.

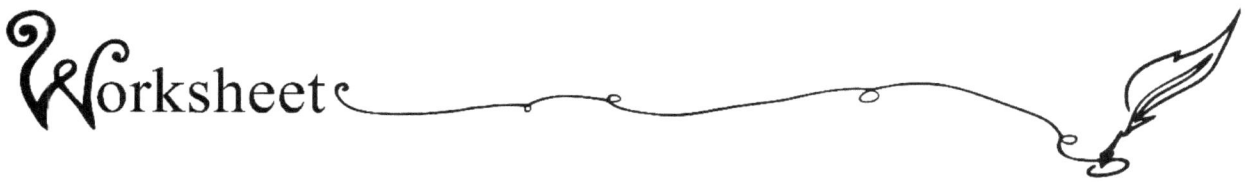

## 3.1: Choose your ordering strategy

Decide on a strategy that works for you, your writing style, and your manuscript.

**Consider the above three options** to order the elements in your manuscript. What strikes you as the pros and cons of each option? Does one immediately appeal to you, and if so, does it match your habits or natural writing style?

**Write your thoughts below.** You can change strategies as needed; give yourself time for reflection if and when you do.

# Using Technology to Help

It's become so commonplace to generate text by working directly in word processing software (Word, Pages, Google Docs) that writing longhand now seems quaint. Eventually, though, if you expect to publish, your manuscript will need to be in a digitized form.

The good news is that you no longer need to type as you write. For many people, that freedom is a real advantage. Tools are available to help get your words into electronic form to be easily shared and edited. The cost of such tools runs from free to hundreds of dollars. Only you can decide if the price is worth it, compared to the time those tools will save you, given the traditional alternatives.

Here are some suggestions:

- Start with pen and paper, then use a smartphone app like Pen-to-Print to scan your pages and convert them to editable text.

- Write longhand on an electronic handwriting device, such as a reMarkable tablet. Then use the convert-to-text feature and email the text to yourself.

- Write longhand in a special notebook using a Smart Pen. Again, use the convert-to-text feature and send yourself the digitized text.

- Dictate material to a voice memo app on your smartphone, then upload it to your computer and run it through a transcription app such as Descript.

- Take advantage of the built-in Speech-to-text feature in Microsoft Word and Google Docs. It turns your dictation into text and offers voice commands for editing.

- Run your draft through Grammarly to clean up spelling and grammar.

- While using Grammarly, check to ensure you're writing at a level that resonates with your audience or meets your target market. Marketing experts now say that unless your readership is literary, college-educated, or scholarly, writing at a 3rd- to 5th-grade level is generally recommended.

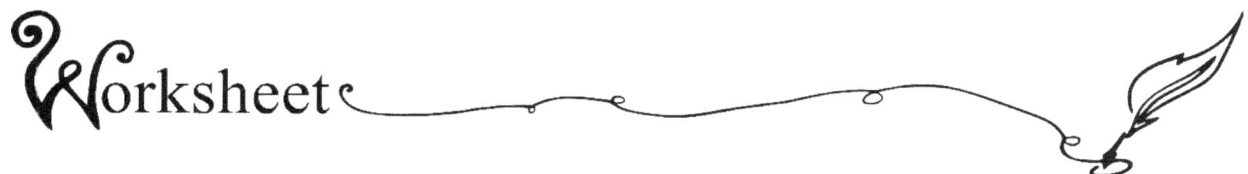

## 3.2: Consider adopting writing technology

**Check out the hardware and software** mentioned above to determine which is most accessible, appealing, and within your budget. Make notes about what you want to try out and why. Later, come back to those notes and write up your conclusions.

## Writing with Chronic Conditions

Do you fear that living with a chronic condition will impact your ability to write your book? If you have a serious health diagnosis, persistent mental health or substance-use challenges, or you are providing care for a loved one with a disability, meaningful activities like writing can contribute to restorative processes and well-being. Long-term goals can be a well-spring of inspiration, hope, and focus — all while managing the demands that come with chronic conditions.

Having personalized strategies and using technology creatively may minimize the impacts of chronic conditions on your writing. They can also help you sustain the energy you need to complete fulfilling projects, like your book. The question becomes how to find the right technology and use it effectively when trying to write and live with a chronic condition, and the limitations the condition imposes. Lana gives us a glimpse into her efforts to balance those complex needs.

## Lana's Experience

*Because I live with a chronic condition (Multiple Sclerosis), I am especially interested in how writing intertwines with healing and health. Everyone experiences adversity, yet we can turn to story writing to enhance our well-being. We can learn from those who have engaged curiosity, volition, and persistence, in tandem with developing writing craft.*

*It is possible to expand creativity while living gracefully (or even not so gracefully!) with a persistent illness, injury, or disability. In my experience (personally and professionally) writing and telling stories is rehabilitative and restorative. Writing helps us to discern our soul's whispers even when we do not share our stories with readers. I also believe we can live into chosen narratives rather than being bound by our current or past circumstances. For me, this pursuit has fostered a passion for spiritual life writing. However, many writing forms lend themselves to paradigm shifts, including memoir, creative nonfiction, poetry, or fiction.*

*I now utilize technology in a myriad of ways for writing. And, I have learned that using technology doesn't have to be complicated. I use the timer on my phone to mark work and rest cycles, for instance, 20 minutes of writing time and ten minutes of break time. On a good day, I may alter the cycle to 40 minutes and ten minutes. Your energy cycles are unique to you; noticing and respecting them can boost your writing productivity and your sense of well-being.*

*I write a fair amount for local papers, and when I interview people, I record the interviews rather than trying to take notes and listen at the same time. I have also started recording myself when I get an idea for a story; recording takes less effort than writing, and I don't have to worry about deciphering my handwriting later.*

*Then there's the issue of transcribing. Transcription programs have proven to be immensely helpful. A one-hour interview used to take up to ten hours to manually transcribe (I am slow because of MS cognitive fatigue). Now, transcribing the same interview with Otter.ai takes only 20 minutes. The transcription isn't perfect, but I find it easy to make corrections. I also use Otter.ai to transcribe my idea sound bites, then cut and paste my ideas into a project document.*

*Recorded webinars and meetings are also helpful. The rise in Zoom-hosted training and video conferencing makes it possible to watch a live session and take notes later, using the recordings. I retain more information because my attention isn't divided while listening. Recording book-planning meetings with co-writers or editors is another strategy that allows me to be fully present. I can take notes from the replay, at my own pace (re-watching more than once, as necessary). Doing so removes the panic of getting everything noted in a meeting, which preserves my creative energy.*

*When it comes to my workspaces, both physical and electronic, keeping them organized contributes greatly to my productivity. After consulting with two technologically gifted people about my messy electronic files, I created useful categories for folders and files. Now I understand how they are stored on my computer, in the Cloud, and on my phone and iPad. Now I can find my work no matter which device I'm using. This learning process unfolded over a year; I did it in stages, seeking help as required along the way. I have taken several mini-courses on Scrivener (the most popular and least costly book-organizing software for writers); however, I have decided that the learning curve is too steep for me just now.*

*Perhaps you, like me, occasionally feel intimidated by technology. Countless YouTube videos provide excellent how-to lessons about almost any product on the market. Watching different videos about the same topic helps me learn new tech skills more easily. I notice exposure to something repeatedly before purchasing helps me make efficient choices. I heard about Otter.ai from several writers; I attended webinars and tried the free version before becoming a subscriber. While that proved a good choice for me, you might find something more suitable. There are many similar transcription services available online.*

*I have woken up to how much of my time is wasted responding to beeps and pop-up messages. Turning off electronic notifications from social media and other online sources can be done using apps that restrict notifications for a set period from all of one's devices. I found* How to Break Up with Your Phone *by Catherine Price immensely motivational and practical for withdrawing from electronic distraction.*

*Leaders in the creative writing community are aware of these issues. People I look to currently include Omar Mouallem, founder of the Pandemic University Pop-up School of Writing. Omar hosts writing and journalism classes, some of which address the effective use of technology and writing practice. Jane Friedman, considered "the" authority for information relevant to writers, hosts regular writing webinars, including topics related to changing technology and writing.*

*I've designed the following worksheets to help you investigate how utilizing technology can help you plan, research, and write your book.* — Lana

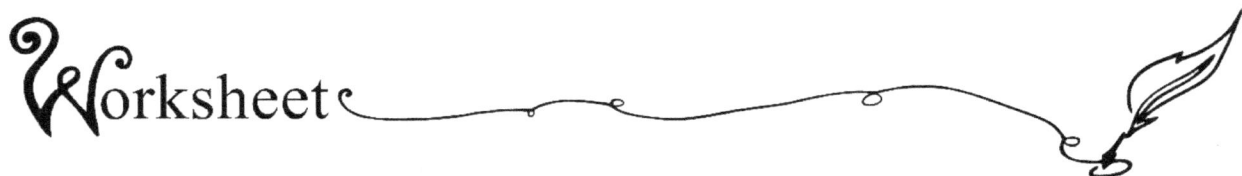

## 3.3: Identify concerns related to chronic conditions

**Use the following prompts** to generate four lists in one-minute "sprints" each.

Your hopes as they relate to writing with chronic conditions:

Your fears as they relate to writing with chronic conditions:

Practical, time, or system barriers to your writing with chronic conditions:

Practices or activities that have been helpful so far with your writing with chronic conditions:

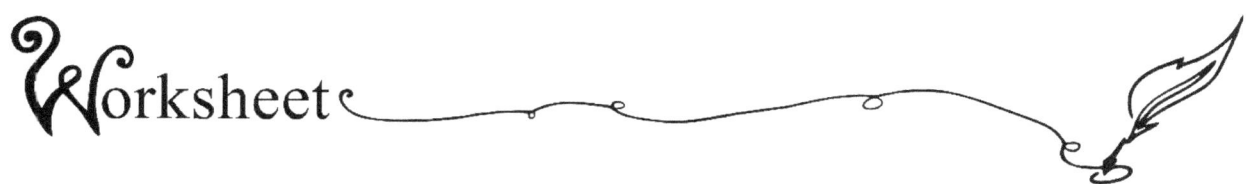

# Worksheet

## 3.4: Explore tech options for writing with a chronic condition

**To assess some common tech options,** explore whether you could use them to meet your needs and accommodate the challenges you experience. Note whether or not you can readily access these items, and where you could turn for support.

Timers:

Audio recording:

Video recording:

Document organization:

Managing distractions (like notifications from social media):

Other (noise-cancelling headphones, for instance, or anything not listed above):

# World-building

The beauty of creative writing is that you're using words persuasively and imaginatively, inviting readers *in*. Look back to the kinds of literature (graphic novels? comics? poetry? short stories?) that hooked you when you were young, and the ability to feel, think, and imagine was awakened. That spell-binding quality speaks to world-building — using elements intentionally to create imaginative spaces, cultivate empathy for characters, and inspire readers to invest in the story. World-building pulls a reader close and leaves them wanting more.

This section introduces the key elements of world-building, so you're comfortable using common terms with editors. The worksheet invites you to experiment with conjuring ("show") and describing ("tell"). And, really, that's the heart of it — knowing when to show and when to tell. Both have their place in spiritual life writing. We close this section with an example from Susan, who demonstrates how to bridge these competing urges — and why that bridging matters to the values that underpin the writing life.

**Scenes:** In creative writing, as in the performing arts, you want to "show" the world you are creating, rather than just "telling" us about it. Scenes place readers in a front row seat, witnessing the time and place (setting) where the action (plot) unfolds, and the figures (characters) come alive to resolve some kind of conflict (comedy or drama). Scenes are the building blocks of fiction (novels, plays, films, and opera). In creative nonfiction, it's common practice to use scenes and exposition, both; in other words, combining show-and-tell. For a lively take on when to use one or the other, see *Draft No 4.: On the Writing Process* by the prolific nonfiction author and beloved writing teacher, John McPhee.

**Characterization**: Characterization is about turning the people in your head into characters, bringing them to life through dialogue and scene work. Generally speaking, you'll have minor and major characters. (When you adopt the first-person point of view, you become a character, too.) Characterization can prove challenging. Craftwork will help you breathe life into flat or stereotyped figures, so they become memorable characters who not only move the story forward, but who make your readers care.

**Setting:** Treating geography, history, and culture as mere backdrops is a missed opportunity. Stories are grounded in specific places, at specified times. With practice (and research!), you can relocate your characters from a muggy Southern church camp to the Forest of Buddhas in the French countryside. Writing to evoke the senses will make the sights, smells, sounds, touch, and tastes of each setting relatable and vivid. That specificity is what you want to aim for every time.

**Plot. Story structure and flow**: Plot is the this-then-that element of storytelling. For some, a great plot drives them when writing ("You won't believe what happened!"), yet characterization truly drives a story home. A memorable character in a conflict-ridden situation forms the basis of transformational stories, myths, and parables around the world. Mind how you're structuring your story. Believe it or not, simply reading your work aloud is one of the most effective ways to recognize (and correct for) pacing and flow.

**Point of view (POV) and tense**: Past tense dominates biographical and autobiographical writing simply because the events described have typically already occurred. "I took the night train to Nairobi" is a first-person (I/me) statement typical of a memoir or autobiography. By contrast, biographical accounts (such as profiles or ethnography) rely on the third person (he/she/they) POV, usually in past tense. "She dared not turn her back to the orcas; their breaching made her weep" is the narrator's description of a woman's response to a pod of whales.

**Voice and style**: In writing parlance, your "voice" is your signature — that undeniable writerly "you," the total of your stylistic choices: how you use syntax, imagery, figurative language, your penchant (or not) for symbols and allegory, and so on. A writer's voice develops and deepens with experience. Your book will sound natural once your voice is relaxed and confident. Like so much else in writing, a writer's voice evolves with practice, over time. Sharon and Lana explore the development of their narrative voices in Chapter 7.

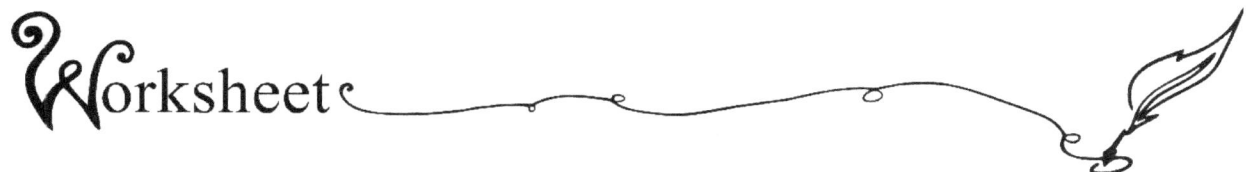

## 3.5: Discover your voice

World-building encourages the writer to "show, don't tell"; so **let's try that on a sentence level.** This exercise is designed to help you distinguish showing from telling, to recognize which comes easier — narration (showing) or exposition (telling); and finally, to reflect on your world-building tendencies. Reflecting provides opportunities to lead with your strengths, not your weaknesses, or simply attend to your growing edge.

**Jot down five random words or phrases that spring to mind. Set a timer** for three minutes, then use all those words in a single sentence **as if you were writing an article** or formal essay. Don't overthink it; just write what comes. Stop writing when the timer dings.

Now, **set the timer** for three minutes. Write a sentence using your exact prompt words above, but construct the sentence **as if you're telling a story.**

**Now, look at both sentences.** Which do you find more satisfying? Which conveys a sense of place, or something about the characters? Which evokes one or more senses (sight, sound, touch, smell, and taste)? Which sentence conveys more useful information? Which leaves you wanting to know more?

Take a break, then **reflect on which sentence you found easiest to write,** and what that suggests about you and your project. Which voice surfaced first — analyst or story monger? You might be adept at both exposition and narration (lucky you!). Either way, the question is, which to use and when throughout your book.

If one chapter would benefit from straight-up exposition, then your analytical voice could take center stage. Exposition affords readers a bit of distance from the topic, to think things through. On the other hand, if you're trying to build scenes, or deepen characterization, you'll want to rouse the story hound. That's the passionate or poetic voice that animates and inspires your readers to care about what's happening on the page. Your work plan or writing strategy will benefit from whatever insights have surfaced for you here, so **take a moment to reflect** in the space provided.

# Susan's World-building Sample and Reflection

To learn how this simple exercise dovetails with spirituality in a broader context, we've asked Susan to do the exercise and share her reflection. She began with a list of unrelated words that popped into her head:

*ancestors*

*mountain pass*

*moonlight*

*threadbare cloak*

*ancient city*

Her first pass would be classed as exposition; here's that (wordy) sentence:

*"We have no way of knowing how the ancestors understood moonlight any more than we know how they built the ancient city, carved a road through the mountain pass or refined their textile skills so that threadbare cloaks became little more than relics."*

Here's what Susan wrote the second time around, in her narrative voice:

*"With moonlight falling on the ancient city like a threadbare cloak, the ancestors wound their way through the cold, steep, craggy mountain pass."*

And, here is her reflection:

*I never fail to learn from this little exercise! The idea for it sprang from an assignment in grade school. Our homeroom teacher settled unruly seventh graders by scrawling five nouns (attic, chair, pirate, bird, shawl) on the board and giving us five minutes to make up a paragraph using those same words. What a humane way to get a perfectionistic tween to simply let her mind drift and conjure, rather than stew about debating or one-upping the boys!*

*Fast forward 20 years, to teaching a course called Writing in Religious Studies at a public university. I adapted the exercise to five words / three minutes / one sentence, repeated twice and followed by a lengthy class discussion. That's when I learned what really mattered: not so much the mastery of either storytelling or exposition, but the students' realizing which voice came naturally to them — really, which voice they trusted most. For some, it was their "tell" voice (no surprise, they were four years into college); while for others, it was their "show" instincts that flowed easily and took hold.*

*What I found revealing was the students' curiosity. Why, they asked, were they struggling in the first place? Why the split between analysis and storytelling? Why couldn't they simply activate one voice or the other on demand? Puzzlement often became lament about schooling, Western culture, scholarly pedagogy, and career choice.*

*Simply put, I was witness to the struggle for self-knowledge — young people wondering which path they should take when moving forward with their lives.*

*I knew that struggle oh so well. The turning point in my life had been a graduate fieldwork course in Pittsburgh, Pennsylvania, where I met with Holocaust survivors, to collect their stories. I was honored, humbled, and wracked with doubt. How could I possibly write up the harrowing memories I was hearing, let alone submit them to academic scrutiny? How could anyone do justice to experiences that defied all language? What right did I have to even try?*

*I passed the course assignment, but I knew I had failed those men and women, all those survivors who had risked sharing heart-wrenching stories with a naive scribe. Haunted by this tension between theoretical interests and real-world consequences, I made a decisive turn.*

*From then on, I would work directly with people, helping them release powerful, transformational stories, and share them with the world.*

*This path has given me so much, including insight into the depth of work needed to create truth-bearing works with heart, authority, and grace. As Victor Hugo says, "A writer is a world trapped in a person." Decades later, I am still learning how to honor that vocation. In my efforts to help others trust the awkward, sometimes painful, process of discovery, I want them to know that the creator of every work they've ever loved has walked where they walk now. — Susan*

# Exploring Your Spiritual Context

Writing about faith, spirituality, or sacred practice and community can be daunting, especially if you know you hope to share it. Opening up about these things can stir unexpected feelings. There may be determination or excitement, but there can also be hesitation, dread, or shyness.

Unexamined hesitation, like unresolved issues, can stall your writing process and trigger writer's block.

Feelings of inadequacy, fear, shame, and doubt often surge when we expose things (good or bad) central to our identity. If you're ambivalent — plunging in one day, procrastinating the next — please know that this push-pull is normal. It's common to experience a gap between how strongly you desire to write your story and how capable you feel as a writer. Even highly accomplished writers experience imposter syndrome. At the same time, it's also common knowledge that the sheer act of writing fosters authentic personal growth. Writing, simply put, can be healing, rehabilitative, and restorative.

There is another side to that power, though, which is why there's also ambiguity about the written word. Lana speaks to this tension. "We writers tend to hold our most passionate beliefs close to our hearts in fear of risking offence," she writes. "It is a sort of lyrical shyness that often accompanies the writer who respectfully summons the courage to pen, and make public, their rich interior life."

Getting past shyness is one reason generative writing is key to the exploration process. Generative writing is where you allow yourself to create, no holds barred. You rant, brag, complain, wallow, or unabashedly hope. While generating, you are deep into creating — getting everything out of your subconscious and onto paper. Generative writing (what you draw on for that first full draft) is the time and place to work through difficult, negative, or hard experiences that might inhibit your opening up about the sacred.

The point is that negative preoccupations can hold you back, and prevent you from telling the truth in your writing. Author and artist-activist Suleika Jaouad says "If you want to write a good story, write about what you are afraid to tell others. If you want to write a great story, write about what you are afraid to tell yourself." This advice does not mean mining for trauma or dark secrets; it means owning your strengths alongside weaknesses. Be vulnerable enough to reveal your unique role in your story.

Every person's story is worthy of being told. How to tell your story is our focus. And that's where craft comes in. Attention to craft means, basically, respect for the form; and it means you commit to practice. That attention to craft will pay off. Your well-crafted work will attract others as they engage with your publications.

The ability to write well is not innate. It is learned and acquired. Craft is what you do to nurture and develop talent.

Bedrock to writing craft is precision — matching language to the audience. Understand who your listeners and readers are, so you use the kind of language they can follow and relate to. When writing for people within your faith tradition, or an audience familiar with your culture, choose language they will recognize.

Pause to think, for instance, about how terms such as rabbi, priest, imam, witch, and guru might land with readers; will those roles be familiar to them? Similarly, how will you name the sacred? Creator, Yahweh, Allah, Buddha, God, Christ, Jehovah, Great Mother, and Nature are but a few examples of how people name that mysterious energy that encompasses the living world. And yet those terms have different meanings in different contexts.

Your habitual use of a name might not resonate with others. Your job as an author is to find a word that does.

If you're writing for a general audience, consider setting aside in-house terms in favor of more neutral language. If you're writing exposition, plan to define what might be strange, or unfamiliar, to your readers. Think broadly, inclusively, and concretely. Avoid using language that you do not feel at home with. Beware of diluting your telling in service of exterior voices, be they familial opinions, cultural directives, or extremist trends (book-banning, political correctness).

Again, precision and specificity are a writer's best friend when it comes to bringing a faith, religion, culture, or spiritual tradition to life. When language is nuanced, reader comprehension deepens. Your audience will better understand why certain beliefs or behaviors create conflict, blessing, or meaning.

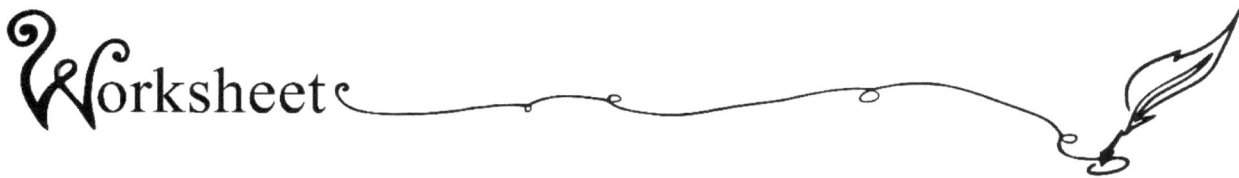

## 3.6: Establish your spiritual vocabulary

**Allow yourself five minutes each to answer the following questions.** Consider Lana's line for inspiration: "There is something about divining and sharing language for personal sacred experiences that gathers community and perhaps awakens the ancients, too."

Create a list of words that relate to your **faith or spiritual beliefs.**

Create a list of words and images you prefer to use to **name the sacred.**

List words or phrases that describe how you **notice the sacred moving** in your life, the lives of others, or in the world.

List inclusive, neutral, or general terms that you **react strongly to.**

Which (if any) inclusive, neutral, or general terms **are you attracted to?**

Review what you wrote by taking five minutes more per question to add or delete words.

Circle the words you would like to utilize in your book.

Make a list of these words and post it near your writing space for easy reference.

## Writing into the Sacred

Writing into the Sacred is the term that Lana coined for including faith or spiritual beliefs and practices in how, not just what, people write. Creating rituals to connect your writing with your core beliefs can be integral to discerning and telling your story.

Spiritual life writing is for venturing beyond the physical, mental, and emotional interpretations of life events to include a spiritual context for telling personal stories. Cindy Van Lunen began photographing sunrises and sunsets following an extended Stage IV cancer treatment journey. She describes her subsequent ritual as a means to practice gratitude and connect with God. Cindy, who also writes poetry and prose to capture her faith experience, says she notices that in observing her daily ritual, she discerns the thread of the sacred moving in her life. Her writing occurs in tandem with her lived experience of the rising and setting sun.

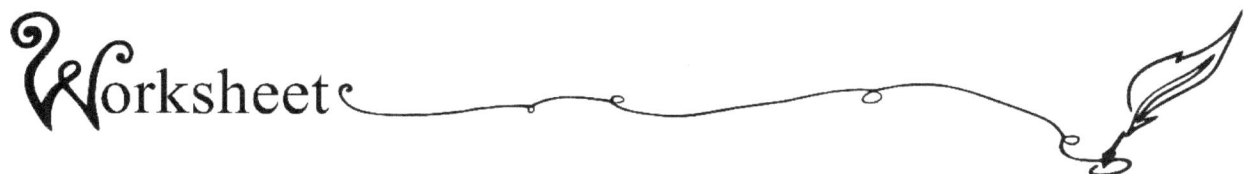

## 3.7: Experiment with writing into the sacred

**Use these generative prompts** to elicit foundational experiences, beliefs, practices, cultural forces, and ideas that inform your spiritual life writing. Reflect upon each of the following questions. Take ten minutes per question to write your reflections. Use extra paper or a device if you need more space.

**What is your earliest memory** of learning that others have beliefs about the sacred? How were they expressed to you? Be specific.

**Write about a childhood experience with the sacred.** How you define sacred is up to you; try to describe the experience as fully as you remember it. See if you can be faithful to the experience as you had it. Then note the difference(s) between your adult and your child's interpretation of that experience.

How do **fears, permissions, discouragements, or encouragements impact** your writing? Write about direct or indirect influences from your family, or greater community.

**What do you wish you believed about the sacred?** What do you wish others believed about the sacred? What sacred practices are you drawn to outside of your personal practices and those of your tradition?

Sometimes we falter in trying to talk about our relationship with faith, spirituality, or religion. Other times these stories come easily. **Write about a time when you faltered** in trying to share a sacred experience with someone, and a time when sharing came easily. What do you notice?

**What helps you to connect with others** in authentic ways? How do you experience listening to others with significantly different beliefs, practices, or heritage from your own? What disrupts this experience, or contributes to authentic exchanges? Be specific.

**What would it mean for you to write in harmony** with your spiritual vocabulary and practices? How might you Write into the Sacred? Be specific. Be you.

# Waystations, Vistas, and Pitfalls

Let's imagine you're far enough along with your project that you can pause to catch your breath and survey the landscape. Now would be a good time to peer down the road and think about your destination. The choices made now will impact where you land with building your audience, the relationships you hope to cultivate, and the readers you hope one day to meet.

This section highlights three areas of special interest to spiritual life writing. Investing time and care in these while your project is evolving can mean the difference between releasing a book that has only limited appeal and one that ignites those many hoped-for conversations.

The worksheet invites you outside your comfort zone to tap some of those future conversation partners for early feedback on a portion of your work. Entertaining early feedback might seem costly now, but it will help you write in ways that are authentically engaging. When the time comes to talk with members of the public, you want the right words at your disposal. Use these exercises to help you be the natural bridge-builder you aspire to be.

## Learning and Shoring Up Support

Spiritual autobiography may be ancient, but the term "spiritual life writing" is uncommon enough that you can expect a little leg work, helping others understand your passion for this work, and why you're willing to go so far as to publish a book. Those "others" may well include industry professionals, because, frankly, when it comes to educating publishers about SLW, there is a growing edge. You must know that by now — you're standing at it.

Consider this: on its publication day, *Body & Soul: Stories for Skeptics and Seekers*, the collected essays Susan edited, debuted under "spiritualism," rather than "spirituality." (And yes, you're right, they are not the same.) The misnomer set off a wave of panic. Contributors to the volume — many of them esteemed writers and poets — expressed concern that their work would be misread. They were right to speak up. Proper classifying is critical to attracting the right media, reviewers, booksellers, librarians, champions, and recommenders. Labeling and cataloguing are at the heart of matchmaking between authors and readers, especially since the first wave of promotion is tied to a book's release.

And if classifying books seems like someone else's problem, think again. Mislabeling can mean a product's absence from the very shelves (virtual or actual) where it belongs, which then means extra work, trying to steer things back on track in the time (typically, six to twelve weeks) a traditional publisher can afford to devote promotional resources to that specific title. Scrambling translates into lost time and revenue, as well as lost momentum for the team that has worked so hard to bring that book to light.

On the upside, a gaffe is an opportunity for growth and change. Rather than lingering on the sidelines with your project, consider stepping into the fray to become that go-to person others call on. You could be that local expert who offers relatable examples of spiritual life writing, or the one with a winsome explanation who steps up to interviews, reviews, book clubs, library talks, and courses. Happily, for instance, in the case of *Body & Soul*, what began as a cataloguing mishap inspired a webinar series that welcomed writers from around the globe and introduced them to the genre. That same series sparked the idea for this workbook.

Start early, envisioning how your book will be received and how to describe it in everyday language that's relevant and fresh. Start a dialogue with people inside and outside of your community or practice. Read excerpts at open mics and author fairs. Host readings in your neighborhood or at your local library. Building relationships with people in faith or practice communities adjacent to your own is vital. Yes, you're laying the groundwork for marketing and outreach, but more importantly at this stage, you are exposing your writing process — and your manuscript — to a broad range of people in hopes of sounding the right notes and deepening your impact.

This early phase can be incredibly fulfilling. You will build goodwill just by scouting for resources and shoring up support. Enjoy snooping in the reference library — and read widely. As we discussed in "Writing into the Sacred," assuming that your language for the sacred has universal appeal can be misguided. When it comes to expressing things of ultimate value, specificity is key.

Start by educating yourself about your spiritual lineage. How do your experiences align with your own tradition? How would you position yourself: as a traditionalist, an enthusiast, an intellectual, an iconoclast, a faithful dissenter? Do you identify with ordained leadership (pastors, imams, rabbis, and such), or are you more at home with spiritual elders, chaplains, and spiritual directors? Mystics and poets might be your natural cohort. After taking stock, step back and aim for a bird's eye view of your tradition. Even within traditions, sectarian differences abound — all the more reason to educate yourself about faith differences and actively respect them.

Seek mentors to help you to identify and place your book in the broader scope of literature. Work with instructors who challenge your perspective. Engage booksellers, media reps, retreat directors, and festival programmers to see if spiritual life writing is even on their radar.

In the meantime, try to work with sympathetic writing partners and knowledgeable editors who appreciate your dream and can help you to fulfill it.

Now is the time to exercise your voice. To be an author is to be an advocate. Let your gift for leadership shine.

## Vocabulary and Values

Words, of course, are a writer's stock in trade. And while you want your world-building to be accurate and vivid, the reality is that when it comes to describing lived experience, word choice can be tricky. Some people easily grasp language around faith, ceremony, practice, or tradition. Some talk openly about spirit.

It's commonplace now to hear someone say they are not religious, but they are spiritual. Some people see spirituality as superior to organized religion. Personal preferences aside, for countless observant people around the world spirituality is a dimension of — not separate from, or in opposition to — the riches of tradition. Writers, poets, and storytellers each have a responsibility to acknowledge these kinds of differences and respect them. Respecting other people's perceptions is a goodwill gesture that ensures these communities are seen and heard.

We've discussed being upfront with your audience about the words you're using, how you will define them, and how the exact same words will be heard differently, depending on the context. The word "witch" has been used for centuries to ostracize, demonize, and condemn women. Now, the identifier is being reclaimed by Wiccan practitioners around the globe. Unless you are tuned into shifts in history, language, and practice, you can alienate readers, and not know why. Insiders may well align with what you're saying. (They may disagree, but they will still be able to understand you.) By contrast, readers outside your inner circle can feel excluded, unseen, unrepresented, or just not privy to the world you conjured.

So, think about your values, and how your work embodies them. For example, if you see yourself as a unifier, (an educator, counsellor, consensus-builder, mediator), you likely won't want to split your audience. In that case, for a big-tent approach that is welcoming and inclusive, use world-building strategies that are openly inviting. Say things in plain English. Avoid preaching and exhorting. Skip language that only the in-group understands. Rely instead on vivid storytelling to get your points across.

Is your humble book project worth all this effort? From our experience, yes, it absolutely is. The inclusivity you seek begins and ends with what rolls off the tongue. Remember, your book is your creation. You have the power to make it sing.

## Do No Harm

Do no harm. What could be a more ethical, fair-minded goal? And yet, do we always know when we're engaged in harmful practices? What seems reasonable in one setting might well be insulting in another. Language often circulates in ways that reinforce stereotypes or biases, or that perpetuate something that a group wants stopped, an image they want to shed.

A modest, but instructive, example is when The Church of Jesus Christ of Latter-day Saints updated its style guide to discontinue the use of "Mormon" or "LDS" when reporting on the church. That's quite an ask for the public, considering members have been calling themselves Mormon since the 1830s. What began as common slang for a religious group (much like Baptist or Methodist) became a label proudly claimed by millions the world over. The Church even ran a wildly successful "I am a Mormon" marketing campaign. But with that 2018 mandate issued by Church leadership, anyone writing about the denomination now has to make an informed choice: comply, or not, with the institution's wishes.

See how values inform a writer's choice even at the sentence level? Mormon and Mormonism are words with such traction in popular culture, they're not about to disappear. In any case, whether or not your average reader knows it, they are impacted by the choices writers and publishers are now required to make.

Creative writing is an enterprise that, by its very nature, pushes boundaries. While reporters are required to adhere to formal standards, non-compliant (that is, creative) writers who simply do what they think will resonate with their audience can be seen as problematic. The same is true for authors who are provocative, comedic, or iconoclastic. Or simply cutting-edge. If an institution or a group with substantial power calls out those writers, they can end up marginalized, their works banned, and their voices silenced. For a proactive example of how writers can respond to the suppression of children's literature, see Chapter 7, "Writing as Invitation," with co-authors Lori Sebastianutti and Linda Trinh.

This alarming dynamic is becoming increasingly common, and yet in a free society, writers engaged in boundary-pushing fulfill a vital role. Certain stories can only be told using pushback, irony, stringent analysis, and outright critique. An author who has left a tradition and is using their book as a platform to call out abuse, is by definition critical and must remain so. By the same token, a faithful dissenter who explores the underside of their community is required to shine a light into the shadows. To silence such authors is to inflict harm on *them*.

Keep in mind then, as you're building allies and support networks, that those who risk speaking truth to power are also vulnerable — less so than the groups or institutions being critiqued.

Those authors will benefit from support and guidance, whether it's the project design stage, or outreach and beyond.

Fact or fiction, truth or gossip, controversial work will attract an audience. Consider, then, the authors you are comfortable supporting. Then ask yourself, what kind of attention are you comfortable seeking?

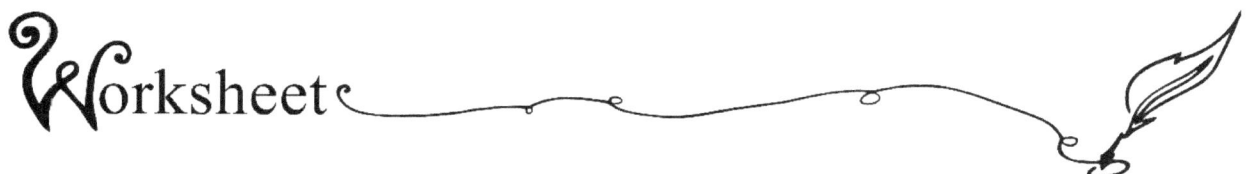

## 3.8: Ask for diverse feedback

Build a list of people you are willing to ask for feedback, including individuals from these two groups:

- The first kind of respondent would be someone who shares your values or is familiar enough with the worldview you describe to pick up on errors and omissions. Getting early feedback from this kind of reader will help recalibrate your world-building while you're still experimenting.
- The second set of respondents would bring a fresh perspective. Their commentary would alert you to the overall intelligibility of your project to readers outside your inner circle.

Regardless of your intended audience, if you are a consensus-builder or an educator, you will benefit from knowing whether the images and assumptions you rely on are too in-house, idiosyncratic, or restrictive.

**Make a list of knowledgeable people** in your sacred community and at least two people from a culture, tradition, or faith outside your own. **Ask them for feedback** on a sample of your work.

**Reflect on the feedback from respondents.** What surprises you? In what ways do you feel affirmed or challenged? If others struggle to relate well to your work, that's a clear signal to head back to the drawing board for some serious revising.

What do you need to act on: adjust your research? Revise your work plan? Re-envision your audience?

Remember, none of this feedback-and-response is wasted. What you find out now will lay the groundwork for a better book, as well as a better plan for marketing and outreach.

# Chapter 4
# EDITING and POLISHING

*A writer is someone for whom writing
is more difficult than it is for other people.*
— Rainer Maria Rilke

*If a book is well written, I always find it too short.*
— Jane Austin

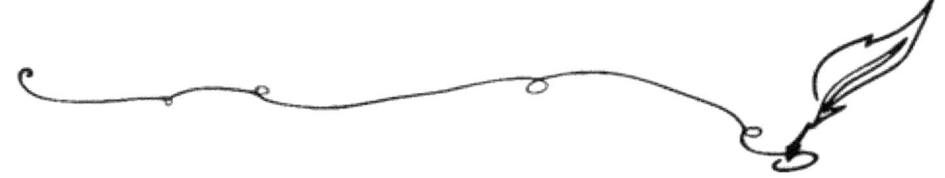

# Editors and Kinds of Editing

An editor is not a fixer. Editors do not thrive on pointing out mistakes. Editors are professional improvers — often visionaries who fall in love with human potential and will do everything in their power to bring a person's work to fruition. Why then, does editing (which plays a role in everything from writing and publishing to film, photography, and fashion) remain one of the most imprecise words in the English language? One reason is that the nature of editing depends on the medium, the platform, the project, the creator, and the desired outcome for a target audience. Simply put, different stages of development require different kinds of expertise.

The main thing for our purposes is to reassure you that it can be liberating to work with professionals who can guide you through the editorial and publishing process. The worksheet in this section encourages you to explore the questions and concerns you will want to share with your editor(s) when the time is right.

## Working with Editors

Note the word *professionals*. Aunt Millie's generous offer to proofread your manuscript may or may not yield the results you were expecting. Professional editors have a duty of care to the author and the piece in question. If also working for a publisher, then the editor's care includes the publication and its audience. That's a lot of care, right? Yes, it is. Editing is a holistic enterprise that works from the big-picture down to the fine-grain to render a creation the best that it can be. Editors typically work closely with authors to bring out the best in them, and to remedy anything that blocks or impedes the energy and message (think: flow, logic, clarity, grammar, style, structure, characterization, plot, and so on) of the piece itself.

In short, you are wise to look for editorial attention from the right kind of editor at the right stage of your project. And if that sounds like a big commitment, maybe it would help to know that even seasoned authors and editors seek that kind of guidance and direction.

Ron Grimes is a scholar, author, and a founding editor of the Oxford Ritual Studies series. His literary essay "The Backsides of White Souls" explores his family's explosive history of religious, racial, and political in-fighting — issues that families generally don't want exposed in print. The essay was not an easy one to write, nor the story an easy one to tell. Basically, Grimes learns that his upstanding Christian great-grandparents were active members of a small Texas chapter of the Ku Klux Klan (K.K.K.).

Along with Susan Scott, his editor and spouse (and incidentally, *our* Susan), Grimes explores the complex backstory involved in researching and writing "Backsides." The pair does this in a separate essay, a dialogue they co-wrote while "Backsides" was out on submission. "Sleeping with the Author" introduces us to two publishing professionals wrestling with similar issues that every author faces. Grimes: How should I tell this story? Scott: What will be the impact of your truth-telling? "Across five generations," Grimes writes, "mine has been a 'good' family, respected in the community." When that family myth implodes, both the author and editor must ask what else is likely to blow up once "Backsides" is picked up by a publisher and is splashed around the Web?

Craft issues also surface in their conversation. Grimes admits he "had a hard time figuring out what the argument was." His initial plot and setting "were too elaborate." But, like much spiritual life writing, this author and editor have their eye on something else entirely. "Sure," Grimes writes, "'Backsides' needs to be artistically rendered, but it also needs to be ethical and critical. The essay takes up unfinished family, ethnic, and national business that implicates living members of my family. I can't think only about characters. I also have to think about people."

The people in this case were not abstract readers, or some far-flung audience. The people who would be impacted by the "Backsides" story were family members, struggling with the very real consequences of discovering hard-hitting truths about their heritage and exposing them to sunlight. The duty of care shared by author and editor is why the two worked closely to share their hard-won decisions in a public format.

Conversations with your editors are likely to be less fraught than the Grimes-Scott dialogue suggests. Even so, we hope their frank example ignites your willingness to raise questions about more than craft. Start thinking now about motivation, intentions, and impact, and plan to think those through with an advisor you respect and trust.

## Kinds of Editing

Exact descriptions of editorial roles and functions differ depending on industry norms and standards. Research your local chapter of ACES: The Society for Editing, or Editors Canada, and ask for recommendations from other authors working in a similar vein. The kinds of editing described below reflect the services offered by our publishing partner, Creative Connex.

**Manuscript evaluation** is the first step in engaging the right kind of editor for your project. An editor assesses the work as a whole and suggests which kinds of editing you need and why.

**Developmental editing** is focused on developing your manuscript. It is a big-picture edit that addresses gaps or shortcomings through feedback about your choices concerning structure, style, plot, and characterization. A developmental, or structural, editor's job is to assess the work as is and suggest the various ways you can improve it.

**Content editing** aligns a manuscript with publishable standards by offering additional support for structure and content. A content editor's job is to take the developmental edit to the next level by zeroing in on organization, flow, clarity, readability, vocabulary, and characterization.

**Copy editing** shifts the focus to a line-by-line level of detail. A copy editor's job is to establish consistency in grammar, spelling, style, punctuation, and word usage. (At this point, you and your editor will also want to agree on a style sheet or guide.)

**Proofreading** is done once the manuscript is laid out and before it goes to print. The proofreading editor corrects lingering typos, as well as mistakes in formatting, punctuation, spelling, capitalization, grammar, and verb tense.

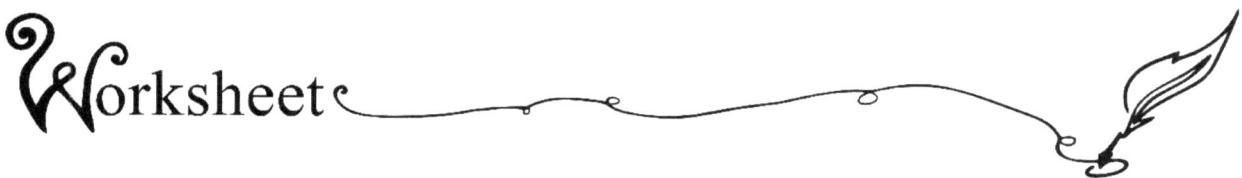

## 4.1: Investigate the editing process

**Draft questions or concerns you would like to bring to editors** at the different stages of your project. Use this worksheet to guide your curiosity as you look into the kinds of editing you will need, and state what you hope to gain from each experience.

Tip: don't shortchange yourself. The developmental stage of editing is an especially rich time to dig into your work — and examine your motivations — with determination, clarity, and heart.

# Self-Editing and Revising

Sometimes people who are new to writing dread arriving at the editing stage, especially if they once had a teacher or professor return their papers with red pencil slash marks; underlining with zero explanation of what change is required; or comments in the margins that shame, rather than instruct or inspire, the writer. No wonder we tense up just thinking about editing!

One couple has combated the damaging "red pencil" associations by removing every red pencil and pen in their home and replacing them with green ones. Why the switch? Well, the color green has positive associations — think green for "go" at stoplights, or the vibrancy of new growth in nature. Just that simple change sparked a new relationship with text. Look for ways you can reframe revising and editing as positive, as facilitating and stimulating your growth as a writer.

## The Power of Revising and Self-Editing

Writers accustomed to revising and editing their documents before submitting them to outside editors, readers, or advisors are usually better prepared to benefit from or know how to work with suggestions. This is a case where experience matters. You befriend the editing process and learn to adjust your expectations about the nature of the responses you're likely to receive. Revising and editing are distinct from each other, although the terms are often used interchangeably. Both focus on finalizing your story (or taking it to the next stage) with the reader in mind.

**Revising** is an ongoing process of re-entering a manuscript and attending to the big picture by adjusting the elements. Think re-visioning — the focus is on picturing the story and telling it fully before moving on to fine-tooth adjustments typical of the editing process.

**Editing** is often done in rounds once you've revised your work and are ready to fine-tune it yourself, before handing it off to an external editor for feedback. Each round of editing helps to tighten the manuscript by addressing any issues that need attention. (See "Editors and Kinds of Editing" for details.)

Revising necessarily involves some degree of rewriting; that leaves structural and line-by-line adjustments to the editing process. Stephen King's memoir, *On Writing*, famously evokes the advice of his first writing mentor to write with the door closed and edit with the door open. That aphorism says it all. Writing with the "door closed" lets you tune out harping voices so you can concentrate. Save self-editing until after the first draft or spew has been fastened to the page. Then "edit with the door open." The whole point is to remember that your manuscript has a social life. For your work to be publishable, it can no longer simply please yourself. Your book needs to be readable, accessible, and intelligible — a compelling read for a "doors-open" world.

If you're wondering about timing, remember that there's no need to draft your whole book before revising. In fact, a fundamental axiom is to let drafts breathe first, before making changes. Let some time elapse. Get some distance from your work. Your attachment to your first draft is natural, but attachment can become dysfunctional if it yields resistance to making meaningful changes that could improve the text. (Naturally, a sense of vulnerability is especially heightened if you're writing about deeply meaningful subjects.)

On the flip side, some of us can't help but tweak each sentence before going to the next; in that case, tweaking may be how you reorient yourself, and get reacquainted with your work. Either way, stepping away for a time can help you re-enter your manuscript with more clarity and the motivation needed to welcome changes. And then make them happen.

Some writers prefer to work chapter by chapter, revising and editing one section before drafting the next. Others revise what they wrote the day before, then go on to generate new material. Even a short break — simply eating or exercising — can provide much-needed distance between writing and revising. Still others need more distance: a week, a month, or longer. Some manuscripts sit for years until the writer is ready to re-enter their work and take it to the next level. So, unless you are staring down a deadline, embrace the time you need to grow into the story you are trying to tell.

## Revising and Self-editing Methods

**Read your work out loud to yourself.** This is a time-tested and highly beneficial technique for noticing pacing, rhythm, and cadence. Reading aloud alerts you to missed words, incomplete sentences, and inconsistencies. Try recording yourself reading your manuscript. Play it back and listen for awkward phrasing, difficulties pronouncing certain words, or places where you hesitated or faltered. If you notice such things, it's likely that your readers will as well. After listening to your recording and adjusting your text, repeat the process. And review the results. Be sure to note anything that still seems off. Repeat the process until you are satisfied.

In addition to looking at the detail level of words and phrasing, zoom out to more of a bird's-eye view by asking yourself these kinds of questions:

- Is there a deeper meaning you haven't seen before?
- Is your long-held interpretation of a story still valid in light of changes in your worldview?
- Have you missed crucial parts of the story?
- Do some spots or characters need developing (for instance, for thematic reasons)?

- Notice what feelings and bodily sensations arise as you read. What are they telling you? Do they match how you want your reader to feel?
- Does your choice of tense, POV, and setting have the desired effect?

With time and practice, you may begin to discern the story's own voice. It might seem hard to imagine that happening, but at some point, the story will take on a life of its own, and you will know it when it does.

## How Do Revising and Self-editing Relate to Spirituality?

The answer to that question may well depend on your interest in practices in your tradition that can help you access, or ascertain, the deeper meanings in a text. Here, we introduce an adapted form of Lectio Divina ("divine reading") for listening for "the story that wants to be told" within your work. Historically, this centuries-old Christian practice was used by monks and nuns in contemplating scripture. Many people now use this method to listen to "the ear of the heart" by following these four steps:

1. Read: a passage of scripture is read.
2. Meditate: the meaning of the passage is reflected upon.
3. Pray: prayer is offered in response to the passage.
4. Contemplate: rest in the presence of God, allowing the Holy Spirit to speak to the heart.

The art of contemplation is familiar enough to many writers, and to poets, in particular. If a contemplative method appeals to you, consider this literary adaptation of Lectio Divina. Or, develop a meaningful exercise of your own.

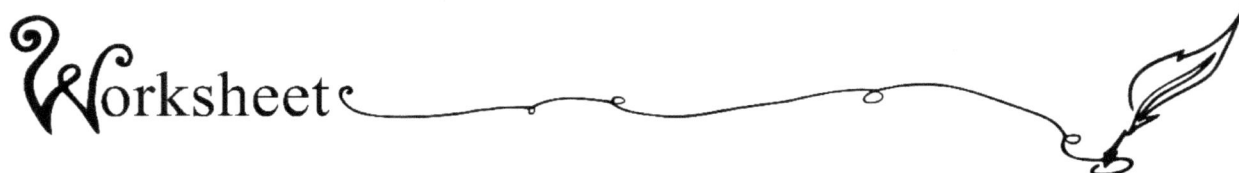

### 4.2: A contemplative method for your practice

**Select a passage from your manuscript** and practice these steps:

1. Read your passage slowly, pausing between sentences. A full breath after each sentence will help to slow the pace.
2. Meditate and reflect upon the passage's meaning by focusing on the passage as a whole. Read the passage aloud. Play with repetition as a focusing technique.
3. Rest in sacred silence, meditation, or prayer about the reading.

4. Contemplate, listening for "the ear of your heart." Be attentive to new words, phrases, or images that surface in your mind. You may think of this as this mulling; whatever you call this time, use it to discern possible changes you may need to make to the text or the story.

Don't worry if, at first, nothing seems to happen. Contemplation is not a quick fix; it is a practice of deep attentiveness that develops and enriches the practitioner over time. Re-visit this technique whenever you feel something is missing from your story, or when you're ready to receive, or revisit, your work at a deeper level.

**Make notes about your insights.**

## 4.3: Plan for revising and self-editing

**Contemplate three things you know would benefit your manuscript.** Like deepening characterization or revisiting the plot points. Examples of self-editing may include identifying repeated words (we all have favorite words we tend to overuse), making sure your verb tenses agree, and ensuring themes have continuity.

1.

2.

3.

**Make a simple plan for addressing each of these elements:**

1.


2.


3.


Try this plan before moving on to other elements needing fresh attention. The point here is to train yourself to notice one element at a time, much like tracking consistency with point of view. Tracking elements provides direction with your next (and next) revisions and layers of self-editing.

# Incorporating Ritual into Your Practice

Many writers swear by certain habits. These may be dead serious or quirky, but favorite habits often become rituals that help a writer overcome resistance to getting into the flow. Working at the same desk, or writing consistently at a certain time of day, are common; so is using a favorite pen or keyboard or simply journaling before jumping on screen. Cultivating personal rituals helps you to establish structure, and with structure comes permission and a kind of affirmation of the work you're about to do. Even the simplest of rituals can signal to the mind and body that you're transitioning from the mundane to the sacred, in this case, your writing headspace.

Rituals that can ground or center don't have to be complex. They only have to be effective. Imagine the possibilities: clearing your desk and lighting a candle, breathing deeply, engaging in a mindfulness practice or body-centered work, sitting in silence, offering a prayer, playing sacred music, or reading and reflecting on things that calm the mind and the nervous system. Rituals don't have to become fixed or static, either. Try developing a range of acts and elements that resonate with your desire to welcome Spirit. One day, that may be invoking the ancestors; another day, reaching for your favorite mug after a good stretch or bracing walk will be enough.

Give yourself permission to experiment and dream, and to contemplate how to integrate personal sacred practices into your writing and self-editing activities. Start simply, then expand and deepen. Consider how welcoming resources, insights, beliefs, or practices from your tradition or spiritual orientation can strengthen your writing practice. Connecting with spirit is life-giving, beyond simply mediating other factors that sap your energy, undermine your writing process, or hold you back.

## 4.4: Developing supportive rituals

Explore ways to include your tradition, faith orientation, or spiritual practices in the fullness of your entire writing process. Notice — and record — any resistance you may have about inviting the sacred, or incorporating sacred elements, in this manner. Be specific. Remember, resistance shows up in different ways — in the body (emotions such as fear or anxiety), in timing (hesitation), and in exhibiting perfectionistic tendencies (constantly revising, being unable to let go).

Think about **what benefits you hope for** with this personalized ritual support, and again, be as specific as you can.

# Getting Permissions

With writing books, the question of permissions — who, why, when or how — can be complex. If you're the originator of a work, why would you need anyone's permission? It's a fair question. And it's true that in the early stages of world-building, you need a lot of latitude to conjure scenes and characters fully and freely. But at some point, if you're writing about real people in real time, and your story implicates their lives or reputation, you may want to reach out to the key people you're depicting to secure their permission, or, at the very least, to notify them that they're in your book.

This section begins with a brief overview of copyright and quoting, where the laws are more or less clear. It's when you turn people into characters that things get murky. Some writers never contact anyone. For some, the question of permissions does not come up. Others check in first with "characters" who may have a vested interest in how they will appear.

Remember that, as exhilarating as this project is for you, not everyone may be keen on being rendered as a character in your book. Lining up permissions can also introduce another layer of interaction that slows down your hoped-for publication timeline. You need to be prepared for that. That's why we're introducing a couple of considerations for when you're sorting out what to do, with whom, and why.

Along with the worksheets, Sharon shares sample letters she has drafted that give you lots of detail to draw upon. As always, feel free to adapt or ignore these forms. We simply offer them with the understanding that you'll do what works for you and the specifics of your project.

## Copyright and Quoting

We tend to quote our heroes freely when in person. Quoting is a sign of admiration! But if you plan to quote your favorite author (or songwriter, or playwright, etc.) in print, you need to deal with copyright, specifically, whether (or how) to gain permission for the right to use that person's work. So, before you simply copy and paste a favorite quote into your manuscript, check the source's publication page. Next to © (the copyright symbol) will be the attribution statement. Chances are, it says that if you want to quote the work, you will need the publisher's permission.

You may well know someone who assumes that the charming little book they plan to publish is so below the radar, they can ignore that statement (as in, who will ever know or care?). But consider this: copyrights, like patents and trademarks, protect intellectual property. They have been put in place explicitly for the benefit of creators, to safeguard the integrity of their work. Would you want to open someone's book and see your words used without acknowledgement? It's worth considering the question, and not just because you try to follow the Golden Rule.

Copyright law is keyed to jurisdiction, so you'll need to search for what pertains to you. Happily, governments are invested in helping people follow the regulations, which is why you will find the latter in online documents, along with FAQs. In Canada, copyright is protected from the creation of a work until 70 years after the creator's death; the Government of Canada has produced "A Guide to Copyrights" that spells out the details. The U.S. Copyright Office is the place to learn about conventions, laws, and protected usage in the States. Under the "fair use" doctrine, for instance, authors are entitled to quote for "commentary, criticism, reporting, and scholarly reports."

Does that extend to you and your winsome memoir? Maybe, maybe not.

Our advice is, just don't leave this issue up to guesswork. For peace of mind, tick those permission boxes in your Progress Tracker well before your book goes to publication. Contact your local writer's guild, authors association, and related state or provincial writers' networks for the latest advice about approaching publishers or authors for permission.

## Identifiers: What's in a Name?

Here's another delicious dilemma: whether to use real names and obvious identifiers, or whether pseudonyms or amalgamated characters (say, three people rolled into one) might be the way to go. This is another issue where tapping into other writers' expertise will help you decide what is best for you.

Identifiers are significant issues if you're writing about valued relationships, such as family members or colleagues, or contentious relations (say, frenemies or exes). For some writers, the decision comes down to a matter of respect, reaching out to key people they're depicting, so the latter understand why they've been written into a book, and the value of the writer's choice of how to name them.

If you decide to secure permissions, try to make the process conversational rather than legalistic. Give folks a little friendly context. Let them glimpse your plans and motivations. That can lead to surprising insights, rewarding exchanges, and even future fans. The second worksheet below includes Sharon's sample letters for adapting, so you can make your "asks" as formal or informal as you like.

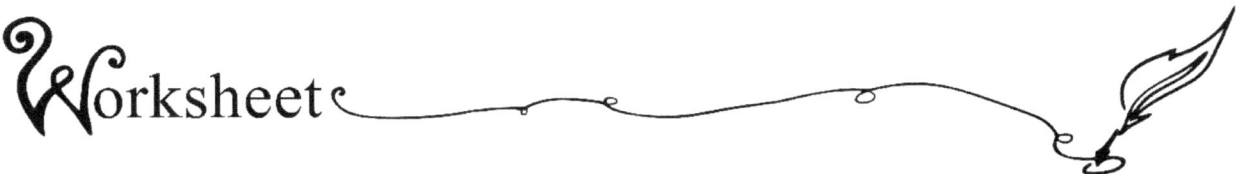

### 4.5: Track your permission requests

List all those whose permissions you need, when you sought those permissions, and if/how the person or the publisher responded.

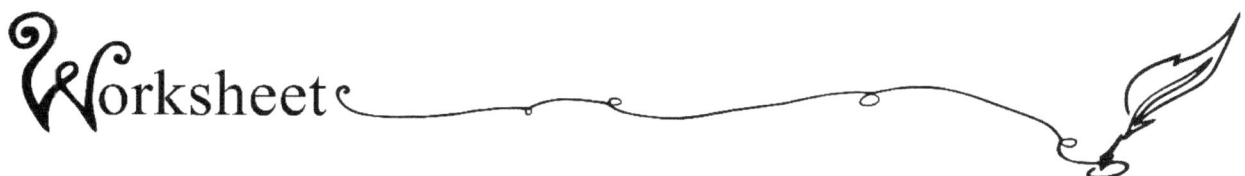

## 4.6: Customize your permission materials

**Customize these samples** once you are ready to reach out for permissions.

SAMPLE DETAILED REQUEST re: Name Use

Date

Dear _____,

I am writing to ask your permission to identify you by first name in an anecdote I have included in a book I have written.

The title of the book is _____, and the topic is_____. I plan to publish the book via print-on-demand. A copy will be printed only when someone orders it. It will be available through Amazon and other Internet booksellers, or customers will be able to special order it through bookstores. I hope to have it available by _____.

In addition to the book, I have started a companion blog (xxxxx.com) and have a Facebook fan page. I plan to market the book primarily with Internet marketing methods, including social marketing, plus some traditional methods such as press releases and book signings.

I have enclosed a copy of the Introduction, an annotated outline, and a copy of the chapter in which your name will appear, with the anecdote highlighted. As you will see, the draft version does not include your real first name.

If you are willing to let me use this material in my book, please return the permission form and attached page(s) in the enclosed envelope.

(1) Sign the permission form, indicating how you would like to be acknowledged.

(2) Initial each page attached to the permission form, to indicate your acceptance of the text.

If you prefer to type in your information, you can download a copy of the permission form at xxxxxxx.com/anecdote_permission.doc. Either way, please still initial and return the relevant text page(s) to me.

I would like to be able to include your real first name in the anecdote and your full name on the Acknowledgments page. However, I understand that you may wish to maintain your privacy. If so, just indicate on the permission form what pseudonym you would like me to use. Be assured that you won't hurt my feelings if you prefer to remain anonymous or decline to grant permission.

If you would like to read the entire draft, drop me an email and I will send you the pdf.

Thanks for your contribution to my life and to this project.

Very truly yours,

Sharon S. Hines

Enclosures:
Book Outline
Introduction
Chapter 10

**SAMPLE DETAILED REQUEST re: Depicting Someone as a Character**

Date

Dear _____,

You came into my convenience store almost three years ago (date) looking for directions. We sat and talked and you put me on your mailing list.

Your visit was a strong indication to me that the time was nearing to sell our store. We sold it in [date]. Right before we sold, the Spirit told me I was to write a book. I finished the book in [date]. I'm now in the process of figuring out how to get it published.

I am writing to you because I have included the story of your visit in the book, and I wanted to make sure this is okay with you. I have enclosed the chapter you are in along with the Introduction and an outline showing all the topics in the book.

I have started a website that has blog entries about how the Spirit guided me in writing the book (line upon line, precept upon precept), along with some other articles. The title of the book is _____, and the website is xxxxxxxx.com.

Please let me know (via letter, email, or phone call) if you are willing to let me use your name and story. In the draft, I simply used a pseudonym. On the other hand, I could use your whole name and mention your ministry. The point is, I'll do it however you like.

I look forward to hearing from you.

Sharon S. Hines

Enclosures:
Book Outline
Introduction
Chapter 10

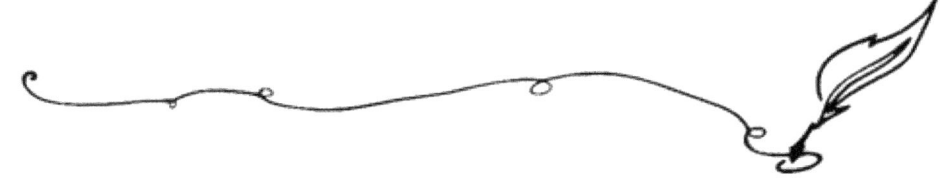

# Chapter 5
# PUBLISHING and PROMOTION

*Some succeed because they are destined to,
but most succeed
because they are determined to.*
— Henry Van Dyke

# Looking at Options

Publishing and promotion is that glorious outward-looking phase where you finally venture into the marketplace. It's a leap that thrills some authors and spooks others. We get that. We understand that when it comes to life writing, especially, opening up to strangers comes with added vulnerability. The question is how to navigate the enormous shift, from holing up with a journal or laptop to courting publishers and creating a press kit. The transition can be overwhelming and it's normal to be a little lost at this stage.

The antidote is generosity and community. If you haven't already done so, now is the time to find your people, so you can step into the light in ways that align with your values and commitments.

The good news is that this is a golden era for teaming up with like-minded travelers. We were thrilled by this offer — that's how this workbook came to be. Steve Sutherland, owner of Creative Connex, invited us to partner with them; some key content for this chapter comes from them. The mission of Creative Connex, to help writers claim their stories and release them to the world, aligns directly with our values.

> *Creative Connex is a book development company helping writers and authors with editing and manuscript preparation. In addition, we do book layout and cover design, as well as illustration and manuscript evaluation. Our team will work with you to provide the services you need to create a publish-ready book, which you can use to self-publish or send to publishing houses and literary agents. We also provide writing coaching, proofreading services, writing workshops, seminars, webinars and more.* — Steve Sutherland

Steve's goodwill, and people-oriented team, have made this workbook a reality. Naturally, how you decide to publish and promote your work is up to you. But to get your manuscript into the hands of avid readers in ways that support your need to be authentic, you'll need to make nice with a lot of marketplace pragmatics. If you're a first-time author, you may have never even thought about any of these considerations.

So, prepare to build a team. As you work through this chapter's exercises, think about how the subject matter of your book resonates with the branding, publishing, and promotional choices you are making. If sales and marketing aren't exactly in your wheelhouse, give yourself time to learn the norms and industry lingo. Move at your own pace, keeping an eye out for allies. People who thrive in this bustling world often excel at helping others do the same (looking at you, Steve).

And remember, spiritual life writing will still be new to many people. Get ready to explain it on podcasts and at kitchen tables. Opening up about a subject often seen as private will puzzle some folks. Others will gravitate to you for that very reason. So, as you inch towards your book launch, practice picturing your audience as an engaged, caring, and informed community.

Your supporters are your natural promoters. So, instead of dreading pounding the pavement, embrace sharing, and the hospitality side of marketing. After centuries of exclusivity, the book publishing industry finally acknowledges a diversity of voices and supports diverse publishing pathways. Now is the time to make your voice heard.

## Assessing Author Platform

If you've already ventured into book publishing, you've likely come up against the question: what is your author platform? A platform isn't static; it's the sum of all the ways and all the places readers might find you, or recognize you as an authority. Having a platform signals that you're worth people's time and attention. Chances are you already have one. For someone in ministry, that could simply be the pulpit. For a yoga teacher, their platform is their mat. For a blogger, their weblog is their platform. For a speaker, it's their public engagements. And so on.

The key factors in any author's platform are presence, influence, and visibility. Having a platform means leveraging your existing network, broadening it with in-person activities, and being intentional online. A robust platform connects you with your target audience and helps you build a loyal readership. Building your platform begins long before you finish your manuscript or design your website. It starts before you write your first word.

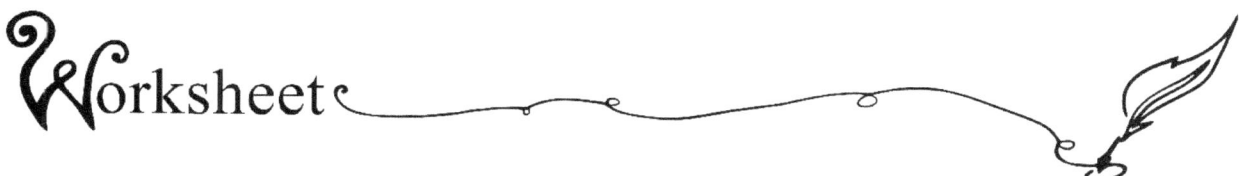

# Worksheet

## 5.1: Consider your existing platform

**Explore what you already have in place** so you can develop your author platform in ways that complement your expertise. What in-person associations and online outlets do you have? Which contacts in your network(s) could you reach out to? What other opportunities can you build on? Do you feel drawn to, or empowered by specific options? Be specific, and make your list as full as possible.

## Choosing Traditional, Indie, or Hybrid Publishing

At one time, being a published author meant being picked up by a traditional publishing house. Now, there are multiple pathways to publication. It's your job as a writer to understand these paths, so you know which is right for you.

Until recently, traditional book publishing has been the gold standard in turning would-be writers into authors. Big or small, traditional publishing houses generally have professional editors, a production crew, publicists, and a contract with an established distributor that networks with booksellers. Large houses can remain large because they include commercially successful genres (romance, mystery, crime, cookbooks). The smaller presses are niche (literary, for example), and often enjoy support from universities or grantors. That support means small publishers can risk signing unknown writers and showcasing innovative work that goes on to win prestigious prizes and shape the publishing landscape.

Self-publishing has been a huge shake-up in publishing. If you remember when that option first appeared, then you'll know that so-called vanity publishing implied that the author had failed to attract a real publisher. This assumption is no longer valid. Indie (aka self-) publishing is now an intentional choice even by seasoned authors. And with the steady rise of popular indie writers, even the bigger houses now acquire publishing rights from independent (un-signed) authors who demonstrate impressive sales.

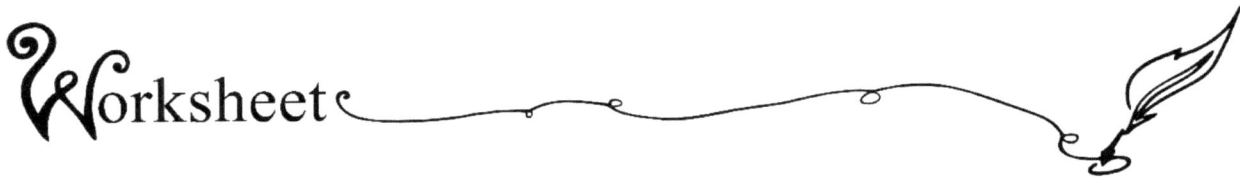

## 5.2: Identify your publishing preferences

**Take stock of your resources, capacity, and interests** — before drafting your publishing or agent wish list.

- ☐ I have the time, energy, and skills to research how to self-publish my book.
- ☐ I want to retain full creative control over publishing and marketing.
- ☐ Retaining the majority (typically 70%) of royalties from book sales is important to me.
- ☐ I am committed to being solely responsible for marketing my book, even if that means hiring a publicist.
- ☐ I want my book published as soon as possible (within a year).
- ☐ I want to have a say in the design but I am okay with having an expert steer the direction of the book's design and production.
- ☐ I have too many other demands on my time to take on self-publishing.
- ☐ I am fine with getting 35-50% of the royalties generated by book sales.
- ☐ I want access to traditional publisher's expertise, reach, and prestige. And I want their support with distribution.
- ☐ I am willing to draft a book proposal and a query letter, and am actively building my publishing credits to attract a traditional publisher.
- ☐ I will likely face multiple rejections before a publisher accepts my manuscript, and I am okay with this.
- ☐ I realize that I may need to sign with an agent before I can submit to certain publishers, and I am willing to work to attract one.
- ☐ Making revisions to satisfy a traditional publisher is standard practice, and I am fine with that.
- ☐ I am willing to sacrifice a higher percentage of royalties because traditional publishing will likely generate a higher sales rate than I might manage independently.

- ☐ The publication timeline is not an issue; I don't mind waiting (possibly two or three years) for my book to appear.

- ☐ I understand that all publishing avenues require my full commitment to marketing my book.

Notice where the majority of your responses lie. If most of the boxes you checked are in the first third of the list, you may be suited to indie or self-publishing. Hybrid publishing might be more compatible if your responses are clustered toward the middle of the list. If your marked boxes sit in the bottom third, consider investigating traditional publishing, including trying to attract an agent. But what if your ticked boxes are in a random pattern? You likely need to do more research before making a final decision.

Regardless of the patterns, see what other authors say about their experiences with different publishing options. (The industry is changing fast, so the more current those experiences are, the more relevant.) Writing associations, guilds, and libraries typically offer publishing seminars and webinars. Seek out informational sessions facilitated by a knowledgeable third party, like Jane Friedman. (In other words, a commercial publishing company's offerings come with a vested interest.)

When you're scouring company websites, be sure to read the Q&A pages and, if you plan on submitting your manuscript for consideration, follow the submission guidelines exactly. Try revisiting your elevator pitch (Worksheet 2.6) to bolster your confidence in talking up your manuscript with peers, agents, editors, publishers, publicists, and publishing consultants.

## Connecting to Community in Person

In-person engagement with your readers starts with a fabulous book launch. Or that's the assumption. But why wait? Start reading from your manuscript at book events, clubs, libraries, literary festivals, and classes — anywhere authors are welcome. It can't be said often enough: word-of-mouth recommendations spring from shared experiences. They expand your network and your book's reach. So, embrace every opportunity to share your passion directly with others.

Some authors network almost exclusively in person and through strategic use of snail mail, phone, and email. That said, it's also wise to ally with authors and influencers with a substantial web presence, even if it's only to introduce yourself to the online universe. A friendly gesture, such as offering to write an article or book review for another writer to post on their website, raises your profile. There is no downside to networking in person, whether or not you have mastered the art of Internet marketing.

Think broadly, get creative, and build mutually beneficial relationships. Experiment with different marketing techniques and build on the ones you most enjoy. Aim to be that person others call on for events and interviews, to craft a blurb, a review, or an introduction, or to offer plain old goodwill support.

## 5.3: Lean into community connections

Get ready to connect by creating your sell sheet and press kit. A sell sheet tends to be a full-color 8.5" x 11" page that includes your book cover, a sizzling synopsis, a mesmerizing blurb (or several) from influential authors, and your contact info. List the price of your book and how folks can order it. Having your sell sheet (yes, paper) with you everywhere you go simplifies the work of persuading others to invest in your work.

A press kit includes your sell sheet plus additional information such as approved photos, short and long bios, and suggested interview questions. All of this information should also be available on your website (under a "Press" or "Media" tab), and some people will want this same info on paper.

**Place a checkmark beside the opportunities** you're curious about, or are ready to pursue.

- ☐ Launches and readings. Attend book launches and author readings to support other writers and to decide what you want for yourself once your book is out. Partner with people and places you admire to create welcoming events for sharing your work, shaping conversations, and selling books.

- ☐ Local media. Podcasts, newspapers, radio, and TV outlets often seek local interest stories. So beef up your conversation skills, approach interviewers, or step up to interview others.

- ☐ Book clubs. Connect directly with avid readers; look for beta readers for your manuscript; showcase your project and ignite meaningful conversations about your work.

- ☐ Libraries. Your local branches are ideal community partners for reading sessions, offering public talks about your expertise, or hosting writing events and mini-courses connected to your book.

- ☐ Reading circles interact directly with your audience by hosting intimate readings at home or in community spaces. Think of bookstores, community centers, or local interest groups related to the subject of your book.

- Book shows, fairs, festivals, and writing retreats. Look for seasonal or intimate events where you can meet the public, autograph copies of your book, and hand out business cards. For shows and fairs, create a memorable booth that attracts interest and complements your branding. To take part as a guest speaker at retreats and festivals, find out how to pitch a panel or a workshop to organizers that meets the needs of their attendees.

- Education site visits. Collaborate with local colleges, universities, or trade schools for complementary author visits (or, even better, a series of visits). Visit your old high school and offer presentations related to your book (for instance, how to craft a memoir). Often institutions will market your session on their websites or in-house bulletin boards.

- Public markets and pop-up events in your community can be worthwhile places to introduce yourself. Partner with another local author to rent a booth at a fall fair, weekend market, or tournament venue.

- Writing courses, workshops, and seminars. Remember those favorite authors and writing instructors who have impacted you. Reach out in appreciation to those you admire and let them know what you are up to. They will value your thoughtfulness and may include you or mention your work in their next offering.

# Establishing Your Online Presence

## Offering an Online Newsletter

Newsletters connect you with your readers without leaving the comfort of your home. First, of course, you need to identify compatible readers. Start by creating an e-list of potential readers (and prospective customers) in your network before your book is published, and even before your website goes live.

Develop the habit of inviting everyone you meet to join your list. (Use a spreadsheet to keep track of names, email addresses, and where or how you know the person.) Sending out regular newsletters lays the groundwork for more formalized promotion and book sales. Informative, engaging newsletters, like great blog posts, pique curiosity and generate enthusiasm. In turn, this translates into support for your book release.

An excellent resource to check out is Substack, which has streamlined the process of creating and sending newsletters. Substack is an efficient medium for writers who want to convert general reading interest into paid subscribers or book purchasers. Substack is also a place where you can gain skills and confidence for managing a website before developing your own. And, when it comes to your website, once it goes live, see if you can integrate a newsletter sign-up form on your site that offers exclusive updates, sneak peeks, and promotions.

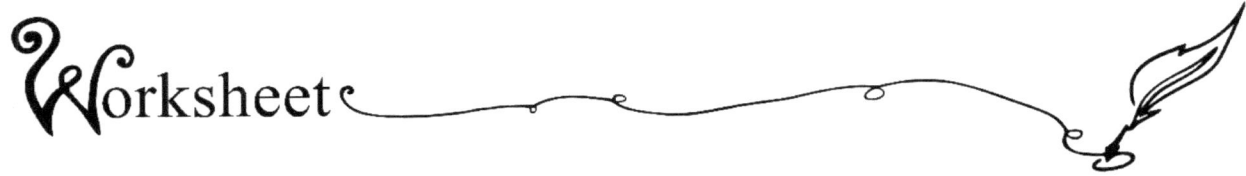

## 5.4: Choose some newsletter topics

Newsletters tend to contain, well, news, but that covers a lot of ground. And, just like a newspaper, sometimes they contain essays or stories. Below are some typical categories of content you might want to include in your newsletter.

**Check the categories you want to try first.** Add others you think of on the lines below. The beauty of a newsletter is that you can change up the categories as often as you like.

**Keep track of your content on a spreadsheet,** with dates, feedback received, etc. Use this information to guide your decisions about what types of content to include in the future. Look for content you enjoy writing, and your readers find valuable.

- ☐ Books you're reading now
- ☐ Ask a question (open-ended or in a poll)
- ☐ Blog posts or sample chapters
- ☐ Behind-the-scenes info
- ☐ Updates (personal or book-related)
- ☐ Discounts and giveaways
- ☐ Upcoming events/appearances
- ☐ Glimpses of your writing process

# Building an Author Website

In today's digital age, a strong online presence is key to connecting with readers and promoting your book effectively. Picture your website as the virtual home for your book(s) and all your writerly activities. Make it that one-stop destination where readers can learn more about you, your creative process, and your captivating stories.

Include a landing page for each book you publish as part of your website design. This is the equivalent of your sell sheet (see Worksheet 5.3). Feature your book cover, an engaging synopsis, and blurbs (endorsements) from fans and influencers. Include your contact info. Tell visitors how/where they can buy the book (and link to your book's Amazon page, etc., as relevant).

As mentioned, you should also include a page for your press kit. (Note that this page is more generic and not limited to one specific book.) Include short and long bios, social media links, links to approved photos, sample questions, and links to past interviews.

The platforms for creating websites are diverse, including a range of free and paid options.

**Free Sites** are ideal for beginners.

- Platforms such as WordPress.com, Wix, Medium, and Substack offer free plans with basic features.

- Depending on the format you choose, free sites limit customization. Even so, they are perfect for budget-minded writers. Most companies offer landing page or full site options.

- You will need to register your domain name for an annual fee (most authors have their name prominently featured in their web address) after which you then redirect traffic to a free site. This strategy avoids (or defers) the burden of building and maintaining your site but still "locks in" your domain name.

- If you're a do-it-yourselfer (DIY) with technology, you might enjoy learning WordPress or Weebly and managing your site without paying someone else.

**Paid Sites** provide more control and customization options.

- Platforms such as WordPress.org (self-hosted), Squarespace, and Shopify offer advanced features for a website with a polished, professional look.

- Paid sites are recommended for authors looking to invest in a personalized and unique online space.

- Marketing experts also recommend paid sites to shield established authors from the vagaries of software platforms that have been known to disappear.

- If building your site doesn't appeal, look for web design companies (e.g., Authorbytes.com) that work exclusively with authors.

### 5.5: Find creative ideas for your website

**Visit a range of author websites. Draft a short list of those you most admire** and note specifically what draws you in. Once you know what you're attracted to (graphics, layout, text, options, etc.), you can prioritize those elements when building your site or communicate them to the web designer building it for you.

## Choosing a Domain Name

Your virtual home needs an address, and that's where a domain name comes into play. The best practice is to choose a domain name that spells out some form of your name (see: stevenking.com, jgrisham.com). If your name isn't available, try adding "author," "writer," or "books" after your name (e.g., goinswriter.com, veronicarothbooks.com, eljamesauthor.com). Avoid adding hyphens and dashes.

Not all web addresses end with .com, although it remains the most recognizable domain extension globally. Think about your specific audience, then consider the range of domain extensions: .net is the second most popular extension globally, .org is associated with non-profit organizations and associated fundraising, and .ca is linked with Canadian sites.

Web specialists recommend registering both .com and .net addresses to safeguard your name from other site builders, and to direct web traffic to you. Some reliable places to register your domain name include iwantmyname.com and namecheap.com. You can expect to pay a modest annual fee to these companies.

We recommend registering your domain name with a different company than the one from which you buy hosting. ("Hosting" refers to the company providing server space for your website files.) This makes things easier if you decide to switch hosts at some point.

Consider registering your author domain name now, even if publishing and promoting your book seems miles away. As of 2024, domains are being registered at a rate of 33,000 per day. It's smart to snap yours up as soon as possible. The cost of choosing a different name later is comparatively small. And since domains must be renewed annually, if you aren't using one you reserved before, simply don't renew it.

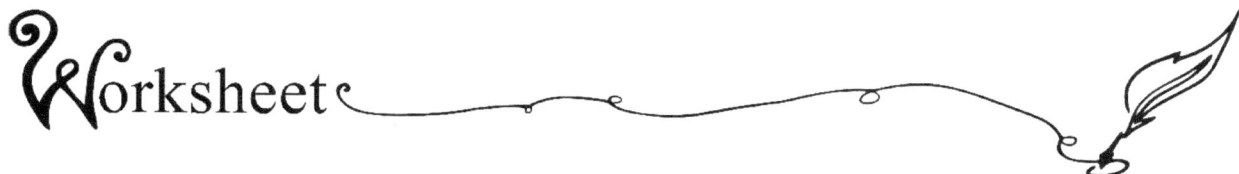

### 5.6: Register your domain name

**List all the variations you could use for your domain name.** Look at the sites you like the best, and note the author's domain name, i.e., firstnamelastname.com, firstnamelastnamewriter.com or firstnamelastnameauthor.com. Do you like the look of an added middle initial? Would it help to set your site apart from other authors with the same name?

**Search a reputable domain registration site** such as iwantmyname.com or namecheap.com to see if your name is available with the different extensions and record the options available in the space below. Finally, circle your first choice.

Take action and **register your first-choice name now.** Then select the option for domain privacy (to keep your home address protected from prying eyes).

- Registrar: _____

- Domain(s) registered: _____

- Date: _____

# Growing Your Online Presence

## Enhancing Visibility with Social Media

In addition to your website, make your presence known in places where your readers are already hanging out online. Think Substack, TikTok, YouTube, Facebook, Instagram, and LinkedIn, to name a few. Don't worry about being on every social media platform. Just start with one. As your capacity grows, join other platforms that align with your priorities and interests.

Whether you opt for free or paid social media platforms, focus on creating a captivating online space that reflects your creativity and connects with your target audience. Use the same principles you used to build your website and maintain consistent branding (colors, fonts, images) across platforms. That consistency goes a long way toward enhancing your professional image and setting you apart. Don't forget to link your social media profiles to your website, to create a seamless flow of information across your online territory.

There's no need to limit your online activity to posting. Practice "friending" or linking with other writers across relevant sites. Leave friendly and encouraging comments. This will build reciprocity and expand your network.

## Maximizing Online Effectiveness

Does all this seem like too much work? You may be surprised to learn that making your website, social media posts, and author newsletters visually appealing and content-rich can become an inherently rewarding creative outlet. Your online presence is where you're practicing connecting with the book-buying public. Try on different things for size, such as sharing insights into your creative process, or offering glimpses of your work behind the scenes. Remember, the more captivating your website, the more likely visitors are to linger and want to stay connected to you by purchasing your book.

Get inventive. Don't underestimate the power of images and quizzes. Use photos or graphics strategically in your marketing materials to streamline your presence across platforms. Create interactive content, like polls, quizzes, or Q&A sessions related to your book. Encourage followers to share their thoughts and experiences in ways that foster a community and promote connection with your work.

Try to maintain a regular posting schedule. Many authors use apps or programs (e.g., Buffer, Hootsuite) that post simultaneously to multiple social media sites. These scheduling tools allow you to plan your posts and maintain a steady flow of content. Even if you can only commit to posting once a month to start, try to do it consistently. Consistent posting or commenting builds the habit as much as it builds anticipation and goodwill. And there's nothing like a little excitement to interest people in your releases and updates.

## Leveraging Online Communities

If you find everything discussed so far energizing, you're likely ready to move beyond your author's website and social media platforms. Here are some ways to foster a virtual community to support your passions and your book:

- Influencer collaborations. Identify influencers in the Spiritual Life Writing literature to see if they would collaborate with you on a project. Influencers have a dedicated following, so consider a project that would expand your reach. An influencer's endorsement can boost your book's visibility and attract like-minded peers.

- Book bloggers' network. Connect with book bloggers specializing in SLW or related literature to request reviews, interviews, or guest blog posts on their platforms. Honest reviews and recommendations will attract potential readers and generate buzz for your book and appreciation for your work overall.

- Online publications and reader communities. Explore online magazines, forums, and communities related to SLW. Platforms such as Goodreads and Reddit have active communities where you can join discussions, share updates, and connect with readers genuinely interested in your genre.

- Additional groups and forums. Facebook and LinkedIn are great platforms for finding supportive writers' groups and developing book industry connections. Be a good literary citizen here as elsewhere by attuning to the conversation first before jumping in to promote your book.

- Pay it forward. It's never too early to support allies and inspiring authors.

## 5.7: Plan for an active online presence

Your online presence is a stage where you practice being an author. Your website, social media, and online communities are opportunities to build your audience, foster relationships, speak up about relevant topics, and show that you're an all-around supportive person. Use the following exercises to gain perspective on your online identity and gauge how much you're willing to commit to.

**List the platforms that align with your priorities** — places where you think you'll find readers and other like-minded souls. Draft a spreadsheet to track when you joined (or left), and to add observations that help you gauge the impact of your membership.

**List the communities** you would like to be a part of online and in person. As you grow into your role as an author, consider venturing beyond your comfort zone. Gradually try out participation in these communities. Again, it all comes back to values, needs, and interests. Who are your people? Where can you find them? What would it take to sustain their interest in you, and yours in them?

# Chapter 6
# REFLECTING, CELEBRATING, and BEYOND

*All shall be well,
and all shall be well,
and all manner of things shall be well.*
— Julian of Norwich

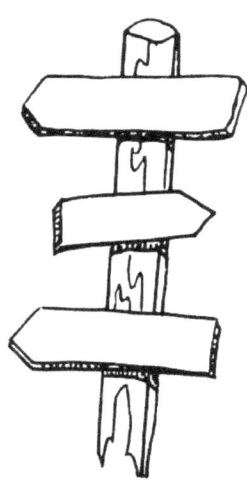

# Reflecting on the Process

Have you ever come to the end of a trip and thought "Well, that's one trip I would never do again," or "I can hardly wait to go back!" An after-trip review of what we loved (or didn't) helps to plan future adventures. The more thoughtfully we reflect upon the trips we've undertaken (and how our trips have changed us), the easier it is to plan trips in the future.

The same holds for reviewing writing projects. Whether you've completed a short story or a whole book, doing a personal debrief is important. It doesn't have to be complicated either, not if you simply focus on these questions:

1. What went well?

2. What went badly?

3. What can I do better next time?

Try answering these in writing, not merely discussing with a friend or reviewing your answers in your head. As much as we all tell ourselves that we won't forget something, even important information can get lost with time.

Cultivate the habit of reviewing past projects and writing debriefs before starting a new project. Even if you have several pieces in the works, a simple review practice can provide insight into everything, from determining the scope of work or mapping and outlining, to time-commitment issues and outreach. More importantly, a regular review practice is a way of reflecting on your growth as a writer. And with spiritual life writing, especially, noticing and honoring that growth is key.

As you develop as a writer, your reviews may change focus from big-picture to small-picture elements. You might release areas where you tend to hyperfocus on challenges in favor of noticing strengths or growth spurts in your writing. For example, you might realize that your word choice and breadth of vocabulary are improving even if your grammar still feels weak.

Asking "what can I do better next time?" can help you identify areas to invest in. These might be educational or skills-based investments. Or they might suggest investments in lifestyle choices, from work-life balance to relationships (mentors, writing partners, editors, community support, etc.).

Use this time to define your growing edge, envision where you want to go next, and tease out how you plan to get there. It may be that you'd benefit from an annual retreat, either self-directed or guided. Retreats can offer structure, respite, and a deep dive into your long-term goals. When it comes to spiritual life writing, any time-out you set aside for contemplation will prove invaluable. This practice allows for a creative reset, and rest. So don't discount that inner voice whispering that it's time to get away. Instead, get in touch with those unexpressed needs that may accelerate (or stall) your writing life.

## 6.1: Debrief and review

**Answer the following questions about your book project,** start to finish. Bullet points are fine for now. When you have time, review and unpack your notes to gain a realistic assessment of the time, energy, and insight you've invested in the book.

What went well? (What fulfilled or exceeded expectations?) Be specific.

What went badly? (What was disappointing? Where did things fall short?) Be specific.

What can I do better next time? Be kind to yourself, but be specific.

What resources (books, podcasts, webinars, mentors, grantors, retreat options, etc.) do I want to consult before starting or completing my next project?

# Celebrating Your Achievements

Congratulations, you did it! You have nearly turned the last page in this workbook. Whether you have skimmed the sections or completed every worksheet, celebrate!

Writers tend to minimize the incremental steps taken towards a goal in favor of waiting until THE BIG MOMENT of completion. But isn't it true that every single step along the way is necessary to arrive at that hoped-for destination?

What would happen if writers didn't wait until the book release party to celebrate their writing achievements? What if writers recognized small steps along the journey? What if writers invited their supporters to mark unconventional authorship landmarks, like finishing their first draft, creating a detailed outline for the first time, or taking the risk of interviewing a family member reluctant to share family history?

What if writers modeled the idea that success and celebration are not all about the book deal, but about claiming our voices and creatively sharing our formation stories with others?

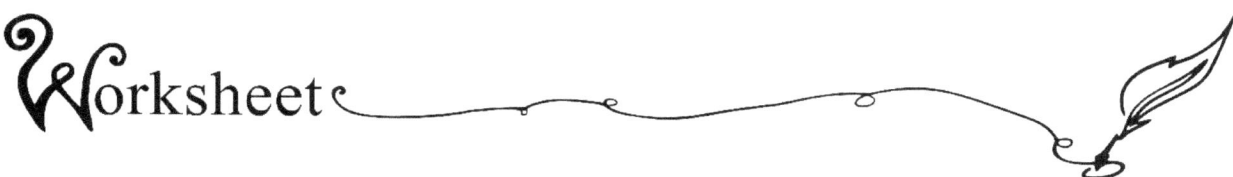

## 6.2: Notice your writing journey

Take time to pause and notice where you are right now with your writing journey. **Which milestones or mini-milestones have you reached?**

Did you discover your faith and spirit stories for the first time, or risk sharing your story with trusted friends? Celebrate! Did you hear the whispers of your ancestors guiding your writing, or glimpse the stories of generations yet to come? Either way, or both, celebrate!

So, maybe you completed a manuscript using this workbook, and maybe not. Either way, celebrate! Did you submit your spiritual life writing essay, collection, or book for publication, or form a plan to submit in the future? Either way, celebrate!

We hope *The Spiritual Life Writing Workbook: From Concept to Bookshelf* has been a faithful companion on your writerly journey. Accept our invitation to savor the moment, regardless of your milestone choice. Remember, you can revisit workbook sections as often as needed to complete your current project or to plan future projects.

So, how exactly would you like to celebrate? Where to even start? Priya Parker provides guidance in *The Art of Gathering: How We Meet and Why it Matters.* She advocates for identifying meaningful life experiences and exploring how to celebrate them deeply with others. She also highlights common situations where people mark occasions by rote or succumb to external pressures with planning. We recommend signing up for Priya's newsletter and her free downloadable guide to planning gatherings (both are available on her website).

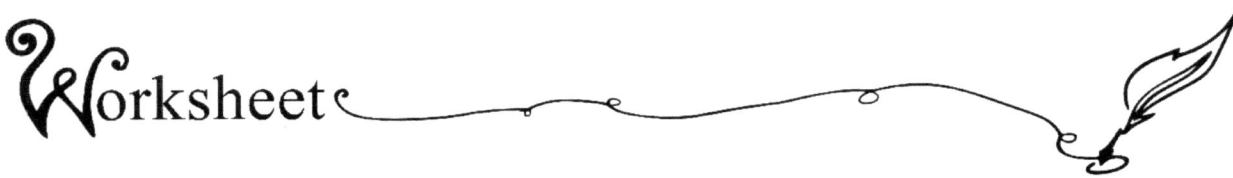

## 6.3: Identify your "why" for celebrating

**Choose a significant moment** from your writing life that you would like to celebrate. Then in the space provided, answer these three questions.

Before planning a celebration, consider why you want it to be the same as, or different from, your past celebrations. Be specific.

Consider how your event is unique. What makes it so, as compared to other celebrations you have attended? Be specific.

Choose themes or images from your writing to inform your celebration. Be inventive and playful. Name a few possibilities, then circle or highlight the one you like best.

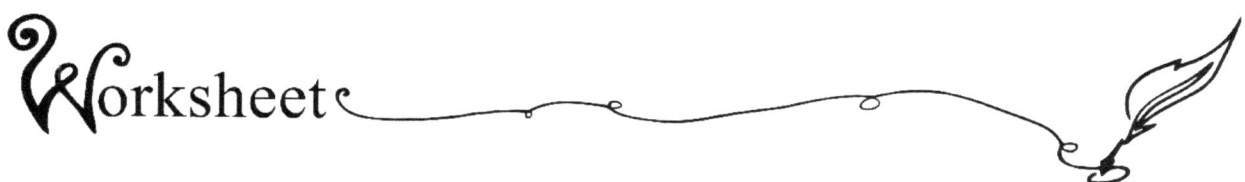

## 6.4: Plan your celebration

Celebrating can be as simple as treating yourself to something special, or expending energy on meaningful and joyful activities. A hike. A retreat day. Lunch out with a friend. Brainstorm several options for marking a milestone on your writing journey.

Pick one idea from your list and **make a plan for celebration.** Consider:

Who will you invite?

Where will you be?

When will the event (if you're planning one) take place?

What will happen at your celebration?

Are there costumes, themed food, or decorations? If so, elaborate.

Do you need help with planning — or just to permit yourself? List possible sources for help.

# Continuing the Creative Journey

So now what? You have gained self-knowledge and writing skills by completing *The Spiritual Life Writing Workbook*, but where do you go now with your creativity? And who (or what) are your companions on the journey? Courses, books, movies, webinars, archives, and mentors are just a few to explore.

While some writers focus solely on writing, many are passionate about additional creative practices and even utilize creative activities to energize their writing souls. Author Elizabeth Gilbert reckons with common trait-based creativity myths in her book *Big Magic* and delves into how expanding one's creative repertoire contributes to robust writing practices. Gilbert dismisses perfectionism and explores how individuals thrive by sampling a range of creative activities free from attachment to productivity or results.

Lana, for instance, explores how embracing creativity energizes her writing practice:

*I notice that tending to plants, refinishing furniture, and scrapbooking are reliable ways of infusing energy into my writing practice. There are days when I wake up and the last thing I feel capable of doing is writing. Sometimes I feel like I haven't slept, so I wake with a cloudy mind; other times chronic pain interferes with my ability to concentrate, and sometimes I am simply preoccupied with concerns that derail my best intentions to write on a given day. However, if I permit myself to scrapbook first (play with design layouts, get lost in sorting colors, or fall into the rhythm of cutting and gluing), I soon shed my fear that today won't be a writing day. I have recently taken my creative practice one step further. I started a designated album to record my writing successes, big or small. To start the day reminded of my writerly achievements, while steeped in paper art, relaxes my mind, steadies my spirit, and informs my writing.* — Lana

Creative pursuits can be social or solitary, and writers differ in how they prefer to practice — in solitude, with others, or both. Alternatively, accountability partners or groups can be a great way to stay motivated. The idea is to hold regular check-ins where you listen to each other's progress and assist with setting project goals. We advise setting small, distinct, achievable goals at the end of each meeting (in person, online, by phone, text, or email). Choose a frequency for check-ins that is enough to propel you forward, yet far enough apart to allow time to complete your goals.

Knowing your preferences facilitates charting your creative path into the future.

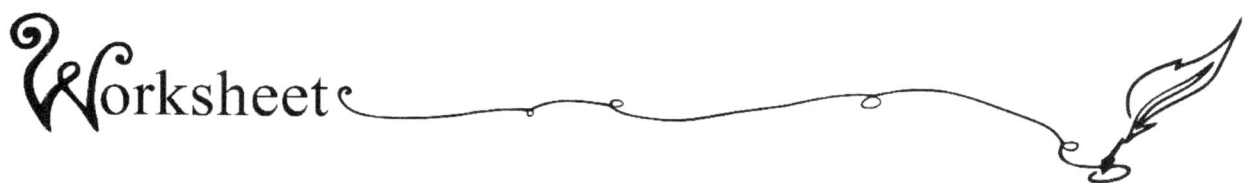

### 6.5: Identify energizing creative activities

A lot of creativity-enhancing activities can be done alone or with others. The key is to strike a balance that keeps you energized. Take a moment to review the following list and note your preferences by checking *all of the boxes* that apply to you:

- ☐ Belonging to a book club enhances my experience with reading.

- ☐ Belonging to a book club competes with the time I set aside for reading.

- ☐ Participating in a writing circle contributes to my motivation for writing.

- ☐ Participating in a writing circle distracts me from my writing practice.

- ☐ Attending creative retreats fuels my energy for creative projects.

- ☐ Attending creative retreats tires me out and decreases my creative output.

- ☐ Group creative/writing classes work for me because I get energized by hearing from the other participants.

- ☐ Working through writing craft books in solitude enhances my learning because I can stop and reflect in quietude.

- ☐ Live online courses are perfect because I can listen, read the chat, take notes, and contribute to the conversation simultaneously.

- ☐ I prefer to watch recorded class sessions because I can pay better attention to what is being taught and take as much time as I need for processing and note-taking.

**List additional creative activities** you know, or suspect, enhance your writing practice.

- ☐
- ☐
- ☐
- ☐

Next, pick one item from your lists and consider **how this activity contributes to your creativity.** Record when and how you plan to combine the activity with your future writing practice. For example: Lana enjoys scrapbooking with her morning coffee before moving to her writing desk once her mind is focused and ready to begin writing.

My creative activity:


My plan to combine creative activity with writing:


If you like, try developing daily, weekly, or monthly schedules to practice those activities that serve you and your work.

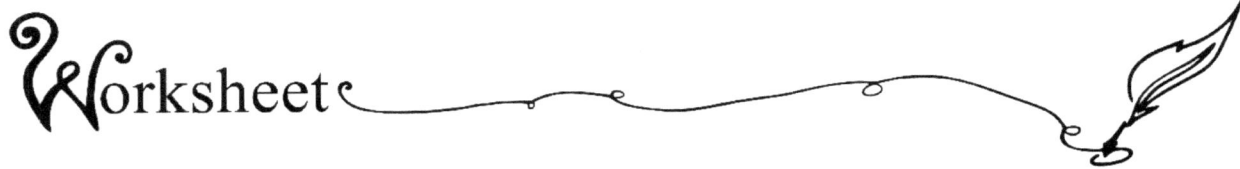

### 6.6: Consult creativity resources

There is no getting around it: to be a good writer you need to read. Reading widely is bedrock to enhancing writing skills, deepening knowledge and understanding, and expanding creativity in general. See recommended titles in "Resources" (on our website) then use the space provided to name three resources you look forward to finding and consulting. Be sure to save some journal space to explore your thoughts about those sources, and where they take your thinking.

# Chapter 7
# BEHIND-THE-SCENES WITH AUTHORS

*Traveling – it leaves you speechless,*
*then turns you into a storyteller.*
— Ibn Battuta

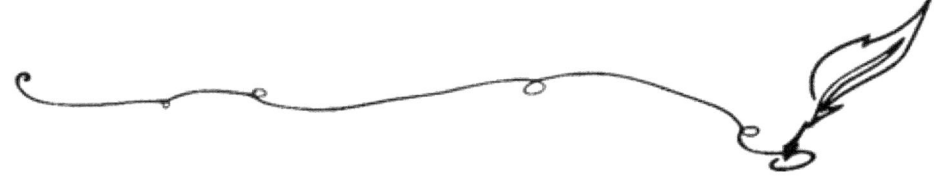

# A Peek Behind the Curtain

Do you ever read a book and wonder about the backstory? Or about the author? What sustains writers, really? How do they keep going in the face of indifference or resistance? They keep bucking the headwinds. Why?

This chapter brings you several voices and a range of answers, so you'll know that, whatever your question or your passion, you are not alone.

"The Truth About Writing" tracks the growth of a writer over time, adjusting their internal camera lens to sharpen understanding of both the writing process and the story being written. "Submitting to Story" is about honoring a story that insists on being heard, even if, for years on end, there is no way to do it justice.

"Soul Work" offers a glimpse of works-in-progress and why their authors remain committed to their subjects. This persistent theme of caring shines a light on the ethical dimension of storytelling, in particular, the desire to alleviate suffering. We see the therapeutic nature of the writing process, for instance, finding one's way back to wholeness, in "Writing as Healing." "Writing as Invitation," on the other hand, is a gracious example of responding to external pressures — in this case, book-banning — by finding common ground through celebrating, rather than suppressing, differences.

"Writing and Resistance" underscores the need for community support and spiritual practice in the face of debilitating forces. Let's face it. Being chronically misunderstood can sap the will to raise one's voice. "Writing as Witness" makes an eloquent case in story form for speaking up, revealing the art and power of testimony and the need for its preservation. And, finally, in "Writing and Service," two authors who have jumped the fence to become publishers say why they care about bringing under-represented and silenced voices the attention they deserve.

## The Truth About Writing by Sharon S. Hines

There's a scene in *Shrek* (the original movie) where Shrek and Donkey are walking through a garden. Illustrating a point he's making, Shrek tells Donkey "ogres are like onions … they have layers." The underlying message here is that all stories have layers. For example, in scripture the layers are things like history, metaphor, prophecy, and personal application.

When I first tried my hand at non-technical writing, in 2009, I was only beginning to get good at reading layers created by others. I had no clue about how to create layers, or how important they are to the field of writing.

I wrote the first version of the essay below in 2021. At that point, I had been struggling to write on my own, with only a pile of books and blog posts on writing as companions. As an introvert, I preferred this scenario to venturing out in search of new friends.

My first manuscript, written in 2009, sat languishing on a shelf. The comments from early readers had been disappointing. "Thank you for your service," from a faith-based teacher with writing credentials. "I just couldn't get into it," from a librarian friend who had offered to proofread it.

I didn't know what I didn't know. And I had been looking in all the wrong places.

I came back to this essay in 2024, looking for something to include here in this chapter. The message of the piece was still valid, but I had grown as a writer in the meantime. I now saw ways to improve, to expand, to clarify. I have put my additions in italics, as a case study in the value of letting a piece rest for a bit.

*\*\*\**

The generators of the workers laying fiber optic cable on my street jump to life and wake me up. *As always, my first thought of the day is What day is it? Answer: Thursday, December 16, 2021. Date established, lack of morning commitments verified, I begin mentally reviewing where I'm at and what I'm learning. Not wanting to interrupt my train of thought, I pick up my iPhone 12, open the Notes app, and type.*

*After setting the writerly dream aside for a dozen years, I've started a new manuscript.*

Last night, I took two sentences of *just-the-facts-ma'am* draft and turned them into two pages of *creative nonfiction*. Stories aren't just unpacked in layers. They are also first created in layers.

Those who come to writing later in life with minimal formal training in how it's really done are lured into beginning the process by thinking it's a one-and-done task. *I blame it on the media.*

Mrs. Murder-She-Wrote sits at her typewriter, and finished prose emerges. *Andy Farmer's (Chevy Chase's) biggest problem is finding a topic. The screenwriter of Truth Is Stranger* proclaims all that's required beyond a little inspiration is butt-in-chair time to produce genius or change a life.

*A dozen years ago (2009),* as far as *this* new-to-writing *applied mathematician* knew, based on most *writers depicted in* TV shows and movies, just writing it down is all that's required. *And, after all,* that's all she ever had to do to produce amazing praiseworthy technical project reports. Clear and concise. Bull's-eye.

The truth is creative nonfiction requires a lot more steps beyond sitting down and recording what happened. A whole lot more steps.

To see the agony of the real process unfold, watch *Jane the Virgin*. All five seasons. And remember, as you watch *Jane* slog through the book-writing process — multiple times — she had teachers, mentors, and peer reviewers throughout the ordeal. Do you? (*I sure as heck did not my first time out.*)

Now that I'm here, I hesitate to reveal this secret lest it deter you from even beginning. God must have known it would deter me when *They* first asked me to write a book. *Maybe.*

In that first, just-written-down-style *manuscript, in 2009,* I wrote that it's counterproductive to know your future. *Knowing your future (in too much detail, at least) impinges on your free will, causes you to choose differently. For some of us,* knowing about this writing reality, *about just how much is actually required, might be a good example of knowing too much about our future.*

*It's an age-old question, really. If you know in advance how difficult the journey will be, will you even begin? If you know a marriage is going to end in divorce, will you take those vows? A relative of mine loves to evaluate difficult choices by taking them to the limit. In this case: if you know you're going to die someday, should you just kill yourself now?*

*That got dark really fast. Sorry.*

*But you get the point, I hope. Becoming a writer is hard work. The journey is long, and the intended destination may never be reached. Writing is more than sitting down, typing the title and your name, letting it all pour out in ready-to-publish condition, and being finished the moment you arrive at THE END.*

*In my faith tradition, we like to say, "if you have the desire, you are called to the work." Just do yourself a favor and, like Jane, find someone, at least one someone, who can hold your hand and show you the way.*

*This time around, I have such a someone. Multiple someones. And it's making all the difference.*

***

And that's where I ended it. Version Two, ready for print. Then Susan invited me to say more. "Just go ahead and take up space," she said. That, for a clear-and-concise type, can be a challenge. Still, it was an opportunity to say what had happened in the intervening years and where I am now. A chance to add yet another layer to the story. And a chance to allay some fears about the social aspects, especially if you're an introvert like me. If the first layer is "just the facts," and the second layer is writerly style, the third layer, as I alluded to above, is community.

*** 

*This time around, I have such a someone. Multiple someones. And it's making all the difference.*

Case in point, my first published book, *Listening for Guidance*. Well, technically, as of the moment I'm writing this, it's still in the draft phase. But really close to the point where I can upload it to Amazon. I fully expect it to be for sale by the time you read this.

It's really a story of the importance of community.

Oddly enough, my first published book began as an after-thought. Here's how it happened.

I began working on my first spiritual memoir the night before those workers began laying fiber optic cable. Finally, in the spring of 2024, I was really, really close to publishing. Working title: *Well Guided: My Life as a Student at the International Academy of God.* But yet not quite ready, mentally. And, I was in need of broader feedback.

"Why not publish on Substack first?" I thought. That was becoming a popular new option. I got busy researching how to get started. Soon I had a shiny new Substack blog I named "Spiritual Life Storyteller."

My plan was to re-publish some pieces I had published to medium.com a few years back. But first, in the interest of full disclosure to my general-audience Substack readers, I wrote about my primary spiritual practice: Listening for Guidance. It's not a super common thing. I didn't want to blindside my readers with divine messages of guidance later on without having given prior warning and explanation.

And, well, I guess the Spirit took over. Instead of re-publishing the old stuff, I found myself writing more about Listening for Guidance. Week by week, I found myself answering questions (FAQs, if you will) about my practice.

Eventually, having promised the memoir (*Well Guided*) to readers, I turned away from Listening for Guidance as a topic on Substack. But a few months later, I revised those posts and transformed them into a publishable mini book.

What I haven't told you, dear reader, is what happened behind the scenes, starting from fiber-optic-installation day. It's a story of community.

I had met Susan in 2019. She was helping me with my memoir. And she had been offering a monthly Zoom series on the topic of Spiritual Life Writing. Over time, I became part of the inner circle.

In 2023, as that series approached a natural close, five of us in the inner circle created a mastermind group: Susan, Lana, me, Vicki MacArthur (a contributor to this chapter), and Kathy Nutt (our workbook cover artist). A new community was born (and continues).

The mastermind group became a valuable sounding board for my writing. And also for the website I was designing (sharonhines.com).

And then there was Substack. What an interesting evolution that was.

I first became aware of Substack about a year before I signed up. Important authors were publishing there. People like Diana Butler Bass, whose books had been on my shelf for years. In my mind, Substack was an exclusive venue for serious authors. Not for little me.

Over the course of the next year, more of my larger-than-life heroes began popping up on Substack. Ed Dale on marketing. Jeff Goins on writing.

It was intimidating, but also alluring. Back in the 1980s, my career bible had been *The Woman's Dress for Success Book.* My motto had become "dress for the job you want, not the job you have." Now I applied that motto to writing. "Publish like the writer you want to be, not the writer you are." I signed up for Substack.

The promise of Substack is that you will no longer be publishing on the lonely island of your individual website. You will be publishing alongside other authors. You will find community. And, yes, I did that. On Substack, I have readers who give feedback, fellow authors who share tips on writing and marketing, a growing email list of fans, a community. It's awesome!

*\*\*\**

So, here's the full truth about writing. It happens in layers. It grows organically. It's a process. It's a journey. It's a school. It's better, faster, and more enjoyable to travel with companions. It's hard work, but worth it. It's fun! Settle in for the ride.

## Submitting to Story by Lana Cullis

> *Be careful that you do not write or paint anything that is not your own, that you don't know in your own soul.* — Emily Carr

My writing instructor's comment landed the kind of blow that knocks the wind right out of you, leaves you sucking for air, and a suitable response. Regardless of the intention behind her pronouncement, "Maybe I am not the right reader for this story," her response felt like a flat-out rejection. After all, the entire purpose of the instructor consultation was to obtain crucial feedback on the revision strategies taught during the class. The goal? To submit to literary magazines before the final day of class. My stomach turned. I couldn't think of anything to say, despite the string of staccato questions that came to mind. Did she judge my writing as undeserving of her professional coaching, or worse, did she think the story shouldn't be submitted for publication at all? I twisted with frustration and disappointment. What was I to do with such feedback?

Not one, but several of her former students, had encouraged me to pursue this instructor's specific program geared toward publishing. "It will be worth it," each one promised, "to take your writing seriously." So, I registered for the 2023 intake of the highly reputed international writing intensive and handed over thousands of dollars. It all seemed like money well spent until the one-on-one consultation near the end of the program.

The instructor's stark observation made me wish that somebody, anybody, had been honest with me before now about my obviously tepid prospects of being published in the literary world. How the call ended remains a blur, but I remember re-reading my essay, steeped in confusion. And how, despite the raging doubts, I found myself disturbingly certain — I would not surrender the veteran's war-torn narrative to the bin.

***

Before I even began writing, a former soldier shared his battle story during an employment counseling session in 2014. It was a disturbing post-war story about seeking employment and attempting to integrate into Canadian society. My role, my responsibility, was to support vocational integration. Our care team's mandate was to help him secure the required services to heal. We failed, and he was rejected for specialized treatment with veteran services. Long after his untimely death, his experience of being denied trauma care support haunted me.

The soldier's story remained silent within me, until half a decade had passed, when I was prompted to reflect on why his telling lingered so deeply.

I had registered for a weekend writing retreat facilitated by *New York Times* bestselling author Mark Matousek. His first book, 1996, *Sex, Death, and Enlightenment*, produced shock waves for memoir writers and readers alike. It was raw, brash, and spiritual. Intriguing. Reader's response to his 2017 book, *Writing to Awaken*, sparked his offering retreats by the same name. I found the theme compelling and anticipated a West Coast weekend steeped in writing theory and practical how-to tips, but the retreat did not address literary craft. At all. Rather, the format was a series of generative exercises highlighting the intrinsic value of journaling. Still, I caught a glimpse of how raw life is reimagined onto the page. My response to his prompt "Where do you struggle with a fear of being authentic or truthful?" came fast and furiously.

I was shocked when the soldier's story tumbled out of me and onto the page. Until that day, my dime-store journal had been a sanctuary for bad days, bad relationships, sporadic dreams, and the odd to-do list. Though years would pass before I even considered revising that journal entry into a literary essay, that weekend with Matousek was pivotal.

The story next resurfaced as a companion illustration in a talk I gave on a snowy February Sunday, as a guest speaker at a mostly empty rural church. My theme for engagement? To explore how communities perceive non-members as strangers, as others. Other than "us," that is. I struggled with many questions leading up to that morning. I questioned why organizations, religious and secular, fail the very individuals they are meant to serve. And I wondered, why not just stifle the haunting voice I heard, provoking me to share? I questioned my right even to tell this particular story.

After the telling in that setting, neither my ethical tension nor the story disappeared.

I don't know what prompted me to return to the difficult narrative three years later, but I sought advice from a seasoned literary editor. She advised me to give voice to the story that wanted to be told.

I wrestled with where the soldier's story ended and mine began.

I did my best to be cognizant of cultural appropriation and revised the text accordingly. Eventually, The Kiss was selected for the BC Writers 2022 Literary Contest Long List for Non-fiction. As is common in contests, only the top three submissions and shortlisted essays went to print. In other words, the piece remained unpublished.

\* \* \*

I began to read writers perched on the edges of literary conversation, modern writers who submit their work, despite the current literary setting where language is under intense scrutiny, and not solely for craft. A setting where censorship is growing, and the fear of saying the wrong thing obscures the ability to say truthful things. Intrigued by such essayists, I rallied the nerve to submit The Kiss to a few Canadian magazines and earned the requisite politely phrased rejection letters for emerging writers.

Then, I happened upon an American literary magazine aptly named *Dorothy Parker's Ashes.* I was attracted to the provocative, spirited, and bold short stories. I devoured the journal's back issues. That's when my confidence faltered. The biographies of the writers all sported lengthy publishing credits. Given that I was an unknown writer from Canada with zero literary publications to my credit, who was I to dare to submit to this magazine?

The submission guidelines requested only the story, without a bio — so I took the plunge. The story would have to speak for itself.

The morning after I hit "send," I received a personal response accepting my piece.

It didn't matter that I was an unknown writer.

Six months later, when I was contacted to approve the copy edits before publication, I noticed that the word count was substantially lower than when I had submitted the piece. The hair on my neck stiffened: the changes I felt compelled to make during the writing-intensive had been edited out. Goosebumps appeared on my forearms as I recognized the paradox. The story, now with a new name, had come full circle, returning almost word-for-word to the original version I first wrote in my journal at the Writing to Awaken retreat. After a decade of carrying this story, I finally witnessed it published — as "Scar Tissue" in the April 2024 Wounds Issue of *Dorothy Parker's Ashes*.

* * *

Upon publication, the lost soldier's story finally came to rest.

It is only now that I understand that the soldier's narrative bound itself to me with purpose: to speak the truth of his circumstances, which included the failures of the health care system in which I worked, and to flag injustices cited flagrantly in the name of citizenship.

Looking back at the consult that left me shaking, I see now that by questioning her role as a listener, my writing-intensive teacher had offered something crucial to my development as a writer. I suspect it took courage for her to invite me to reconsider how I construct a narrative. I learned what is necessary to do the arduous work of discernment. To perceive, understand, and judge those things we hold sacred. To articulate clearly, especially those aspects of spirit that are not obvious, not prescribed, or apparent in everyday life.

As writers, we must keep knocking on doors, holding hope until we find a publication to champion our stories. Crafting this man's story beckoned me towards the ultimate irony: first, we risk placing words upon the page, then we risk trying to find a home for the story with no clue where that home may be. After too many rejections, we can begin to suspect it's our fault — because we are not good enough writers. But sometimes that is not the case. I am learning that some stories carry us, too.

Now I know his story was not mine to tell.

Our shared story is mine to tell.

# Soul Work

We reached out to writers and poets with two questions. What are you working on that touches on spirit, faith, sacred community, practice, or religion? And what are you seeing in other kinds of life writing that gives you hope? The answers speak to soul work, reflecting on things that are hard to voice — wonder, grief, loss, life transitions, aging — and to the desire for a deeper understanding of life's enduring mysteries.

Does any of this speak to you? If so, reach out and start a conversation.

## Exploring New Directions by Dora Dueck

Since we met in 2019, in the pages of the wonderful *Body & Soul,* I have published *Return Stroke: essays & memoir* (CMU Press), a book in which I explored personal experiences, including our family's two-plus years of living in Paraguay. The underlying theme of that reflection was the desire to belong — to belong in a new culture and geography. Oh, how very much it involved body and soul: my busyness as mom to two children and giving birth to a third there in a hot and often challenging environment, and subtle shifts and deepenings in my spiritual life!

Coming in 2025 or early 2026 is a second book of short fiction, *Like a River Divides the Earth*, with Freehand Books. The five longish stories in this collection probe themes like conflict and reconciliation (inner reconciliation, in particular) as well as living in circumstances beyond one's control. I find that I can work out things as well through fiction as nonfiction, or maybe I should say, stories and characters arrive to me almost as guides, each insistent they be followed and journeyed with for our mutual benefit.

Currently, I'm stretching myself in a new direction altogether, by writing poetry. At my present (older) stage of life, the matter of purpose seems more relevant than ever. I'm enjoying the learning and effort involved in this more compressed genre. Once again, issues of body and soul mark my experience: grief at the death of my husband, aging, questions of legacy. Facing toward death, as the years remaining to me count down, demands fresh and urgent engagement with faith and sacred community. For me, writing is both process and outcome; it absolutely grounds me.

*Dora Dueck is an award-winning writer, former editor, avid reader, and lay historian living in Tsawwassen, B.C. Visit Dora at doradueck.com.*

## Examining Time by Hollay Ghadery

Right now (autumn 2024), I am working on a collection of poetry — occasional verse — that explores how people with neurodivergence experience time differently. Also, how screens impact our awareness of and relationship with time and nature. My intent is not to vilify screens or technology, because I think these tools can be used for good too, but simply to examine time, and our ability to comprehend it in its fleeting magnitude.

*Hollay Ghadery is an award-winning Iranian-Canadian writer and sought-after publicist. Follow Hollay on Instagram, X, TikTok, or connect with her at hollayghadery.ca.*

## Reconnecting with Nature by Sheniz Janmohamed

I'm currently working on a collection of linked essays about identity, ancestry, the language of place, and reconnecting with nature. Over the past two years, I've revisited my late grandmother's garden in the highlands of Kenya, where I question and contemplate the cycle of life and death not just in my own life, but in the garden itself. When we pay attention to the shifts in our environment, how does it mirror the shift within us? What is falling away to make space for something new? What requires more tending? What has been here for generations, and what is just beginning to take root? Where can we find sanctuary, within and outside ourselves?

The garden is a metaphor for the complexity and richness of life itself — the cyclical seasons of abundance, nourishment, and dormancy. I find that the society we live in is hellbent on constant productivity and creation, which is out of alignment with nature itself. Reconnecting with nature is a reminder to keep returning to the present moment, to attend to what is in front of us, and find beauty in imperfection.

This is a sacred practice, and one which I hope to bring back to the communities I work with.

I am heartened to see creative nonfiction expanding beyond limiting forms, and as a poet this is encouraging and inspiring.

*Sheniz Janmohamed is a poet, artist, educator, and nature artist who teaches in the University of Toronto's School of Continuing Studies. Visit Sheniz at shenizjanmohamed.com.*

## Finding Grace & Grounding by Pam Johnson

I have been working on a nonfiction piece about my experience caring for my mom in home-based palliative care for over seven months and the intersectionality of that event with a major transition in my own life. What began as an adventure in leaving my home and community in

Toronto, seeking new horizons in the west, turned into an exploration in midlife reckoning. As the writing unfolds, I find myself exploring themes of grief, belonging, individuation, and the struggle to let go of outdated ways of being in my family of origin. It is a story of being present with the slow death of my mother — a powerful influence in my life — and my struggle to find grace and grounding during that process.

I am also working on the creation of a workshop series connecting creative expression with the body and nature. This four-part "playshop" will focus on slowing down, dropping in, and finding inspiration through an exploration of the senses. One of my motivations for creating this workshop is to create community and bring people together to explore expression and creativity as a practice, not just a product.

I am finding hope and inspiration in the writing of poet and essayist Ross Gay — his focus on taking time to notice and celebrate the joys which surround us. He speaks of joy as an ember for "unboundaried solidarity" and a way to "depolarize us." I love how he speaks about the interconnectedness of grief and joy and how we can hold each other during the "unfixing" of each other, the falling, the grieving. Gay writes about the practice of paying attention — the alertness required in the practice of noticing.

*Pam Johnson is passionate about expression and working with energy in the body through her yoga, Chi Kung, and somatic practices. Visit Pam to learn more at pamjohnson.ca.*

## Speaking Truth to Power by Jónína Kirton

I am currently working on a collection of poetry titled, Save Your Prayers: Send Money. It is not against prayers but rather explores how lack of wealth affects health outcomes.

As a 69-3/4 year-old Indigenous woman I have passed the average lifespan for Indigenous women, which is 67. It has been a hard road and so I will use my own story to explore chronic pain, trauma, and intergenerational trauma. I hope to cover things like spiritual bypassing, the commodifying of spirituality that takes place in the wellness industry, and how spirituality can help one heal. These things seem opposing, but they are not. It's complicated.

The challenge with my book will be how to speak about the shortfalls of the wellness industry and spirituality but still leave room for the magic and the hope. I will know much more after I work on it in the coming months. Not even sure I can fully explore all this, but I do have a good beginning. My book is due March 2025, and I still have a lot of writing and research to do.

*Jónína Kirton is an Icelandic and Red River Métis poet exploring the interleaving of body and land. Visit Jónína at joninakirton.wixsite.com/poet.*

## Identifying our Teachers by Betsy Warland

I am still working as a full-time freelance editor, teacher, and manuscript consultant. I work with authors and also with emerging writers. I continue to find this deep engagement with writers fascinating.

My recent books are second editions. My 2000 memoir, *Bloodroot — tracing the unselling of motherloss*, was published as a second edition in 2021. It has a thought-provoking Introduction by Susan Olding, and a new essay by me on what I have subsequently been learning about the complex story of my mother and me.

My book on writing, *Breathing the Page — Reading the Act of Writing* (2010), came out in a second edition with ten new essays in 2023. To be able to deeply engage years later with both of these books has been challenging and moving.

I now sense that I will not write another book. I am, however, on a quest via writing a long essay investigating the natures of story and narrative. There is a tendency in North America to think that story and narrative are essentially the same. They are indeed interrelated but are also very different. In the online world, story (the pitch) has become an essential tool for commerce, political discourse, education, societal control, and online forms of "intimacy" that often isolates, alienates, and antagonizes us even more.

Simply said, each of us has a specific "basket" of stories that we routinely tell to ourselves and others throughout our lives. These stories can be humorous, distressing, alienating and/or entrenched in dangerous oppositions. We turn to various spiritual practices, therapy, medication, interpersonal and political anger and violence to navigate these stories. I'm exploring how these stories are with us our entire lives and how our attempts to solve, dull, weaponize, or get rid of them is a profound mistake. They may, in fact, be our lifelong spiritual teachers.

*Betsy Warland is the author of 14 books, a sought-after teacher, mentor, guide, and a leading figure in the literary landscape. Meet Betsy at betsywarland.com.*

# Writing as Healing

Brokenness and heartache often trigger intense periods of cathartic writing that may or may not make it into a book; what matters is how the author is changed by the healing process of grounding, expression, and release. Vickie MacArthur is a prairie-based writer who integrates embodied awareness, breath, and spirituality to discover moments that expand our way of seeing ourselves and the world, even in difficult times — what she calls "blue sky moments." Her poem, "The Good News," speaks to one such moment, recovering from a devastating accident while the manuscript of her spiritual memoir was still on her editor's desk. What sparked that book was a moment of spiritual awakening just after her mother passed away from cancer. But with the accident came fresh grief and troubling questions. Would life ever be the same?

## The Good News by Vickie MacArthur

The good news is…

the linden tree in my backyard has received a haircut during this pandemic,

a cutting away of old dead branches and growth.

She has come back to life, timidly offering her tender green buds to the sun

to burst into fragrant white blossoms.

She stands in my backyard offering her resolute self, her beauty, her shade, her assurance that life goes on,

even as some of her branches wither,

even as parts of myself die…

pruned away thoughts and hopes of the future I once thought so secure.

The good news is…

I too am planted here, even as I begin to prepare new soil in my garden,

and perhaps the garden of my soul.

The good news is…

the perennials I planted last year are already poking their heads through the soil to say hello,

even as I plant new petunias who will only blossom for a short time,

before returning back to the soil to become compost next year.


The good news is…

the sparrows have returned to my linden tree to nest as they do every year, creating a new family that somehow knows the way back home.

The good news is…

I can still put my arms around the rough bark of this tree,

and feel how it holds me and loves me right back.

The good news is…

I am intimately connected to all that is coming and going,

That which I can see, and that which still lies hidden beneath the surface.

Somehow, I know my way home.

*Vickie MacArthur is a writer, spiritual director, yoga and meditation teacher who is passionate about building community beyond the boundaries of culture and religion. Visit Vickie at vickiemacarthur.com.*

# Writing as Witness

Writing about heritage honestly and fully is hard at the best of times. Factor in trauma, war, migration, displacement, language-loss, and colonization, or whatever limits knowledge or severs connections, and you see the challenge, trying to depict history with clarity and empathy, free from the distortions of sentimentality or judgment.

Trauma makes the need for authentic witness profoundly necessary. These authors show us why.

"I'm writing to provide testimony. I'm writing to give all that I've learned a place to live." Adele Dobkowski, an accomplished professional, was in her 70s before she felt compelled to take up personal writing. In "Pots and Pans," which she read at a 2023 International Women's Day celebration, a modest household item becomes a prompt for reflecting on her mother's complicated life.

The piece that follows, from Kitty Hoffman's essay, "The Chamber of Yearning" (*The New Quarterly* 163), is from her memoir of the same name. Hoffman writes about family, faith, and finding one's place in a world bent on annihilating people and their stories. Open any Hoffman essay, and you'll find fidelity to truth, craft, language, creativity, tradition, and the lingering power of ancestral ghosts.

# Pots & Pans by Adele Dobkowski

I have a small stainless-steel saucepan that once belonged to my mother. She found it, along with its mismatched white enamel lid, at her favorite neighborhood thrift shop, where she loved to scour for treasures.

There's nothing special about this little pan, it's simply very useful, and whenever I use it, I think of my mother.

Still, I surprised myself recently when I was using my hand-me-down pan to reheat leftover chili. Why did my mother treasure the mismatched items that filled her kitchen? Why collect orphaned plates? Why embarrass us by only using relics of the past — like her meat grinder that had to be attached to a wooden crate. What made that the only acceptable means of making the delicious kreplach filling for which she was renowned? Why was she so attached to the old and broken?

It wasn't that she didn't have nice things. She was inordinately proud of the Rosenthal bone china she had carted from Germany to New York, where we arrived as refugees in 1951. But that china was only brought out for special celebrations. It was not part of our everyday life.

Her most treasured pan was the large ancient cast iron skillet, a hand-me-down from Mrs. Levine, the woman for whom she cleaned house when we were newly arrived immigrants, before she and my father could buy their first candy store in Queens. How did she meet Mrs. Levine? I have no idea, but my mother's industrious nature would never allow her to be unemployed for long. And even though she usually found fault with even the mildest person, she always spoke warmly of Mrs. Levine's kindness and good nature. Supposedly, I accompanied her when she cleaned. I have no memory of those times. I was four, five at the most. I only know that Mrs. Levine became our family's symbol for the Jews who were real Americans. Successful people who could help "greeners" like us.

Because the prized skillet lacked a handle, only my mother was allowed to use it, and over time she grew convinced of the skillet's nearly supernatural powers. French toast. Fried meats. Sauces and stews. Everything came out delicious.

Without a doubt she was an exceptional home cook. If she needed to believe that her dishes would be less wonderful in another pan, we were ready to indulge her.

So last week, when I took out my little pan and, out of the blue, began wondering about the connection my mother had with her mis-matched friends, a flood of questions made me think anew about my mother's life. Was there something at play beyond her eccentric affection for kitchen implements? Could it be that she identified with the treasures she was able to salvage? Had we ever allowed ourselves to see the many torments she carried inside her broken self?

My mother's life was a continual struggle to overcome hardship. She was the definition of survivor. The middle child in a large, impoverished family, she was sent away from the shtetl at age ten to be a live-in servant in the homes of wealthy Jewish families in Warsaw. At 13, her father died. The war then compounded loss with the total destruction of an entire way of life. Did she feel discarded, overlooked?

My mother, a smart and enterprising woman, made herself useful however she could. She knew she had value. She was just never certain others prized her much. That pain and anger exploded all too often, and yet even as she aged and grew more stubborn, she glowed with love for her mismatched treasures. In them, she saw an affirmation of life.

*Adele Dobkowski was born in a post-war DP camp in Germany, raised in Queens, New York, and emigrated to Canada as an adult. She makes her home in Waterloo, Ontario, where she writes these stories to make sure her granddaughter knows about a world — and a family — that disappeared in 1939.*

## The Chamber of Yearning by Kitty Hoffman

Wherever I go, my ghosts come with me. I know they are the fathers, going back in an unbroken thread stretching from Warsaw and the Ukraine, through some unknown detour in Germany, back through southern France and into Spain — and back to the beginning, to Jerusalem before the expulsion. It took decades to find the various sections of this thread, to learn where it started, how it meandered through the Mediterranean and northern European worlds of exile.

As a child, I thought they were all from my parents' time, the ghosts of the grandfathers and uncles murdered in the most recent round of killings, in the Holocaust. This was crowded enough, this cloud of male presence that accompanied me wherever I went, claiming me for their own unfinished purpose, surrounding me with their stifled, yet powerful love. Their presence was a burden, their silent demands weighing me down with the mystery of obligation. They needed me for some purpose, only I had no idea what that purpose was or how to fulfill it. Still they held me captive, hovered around me with the constant reminder that my life was not mine alone. Growing up with no male relatives apart from my father, without even a photograph to see what the men looked like, I had only my parents' stories and imagination to people my world. A thirteenth-century kabbalist is as real to me as my grandfather.

You mention God, and I am at once back at the Seder table of my childhood. There were only my parents and I, the three of us locked in our cocoon of remembering. Although I didn't know it then, I was being inducted into one of the smallest societies in the world, those who know what Yiddish life was like before the destruction. It was that world we inhabited around the too-tiny seder table. As she read, in Hebrew, the ancient words of the Haggadah, my mother would add, in Yiddish, "Hitler was our Pharaoh." When the Haggadah would instruct, in Hebrew, "Remember that you were a slave in Egypt," my father would add his yearly commentary in Yiddish. "I know what it is to be a slave." I was beginning to enter the timeless world of Jewish history and memory, where every empire becomes like all those before. As an adult I learned the timeless joke. "Question: How do you define a Jewish holiday? Answer: They tried to kill us. We survived. Let's eat."

I would sit in my own little world, with my own little Haggadah in English. It is the custom for Jewish charities to fund-raise just before Passover, maintaining an ancient tradition of charity before festivals, and in those days contributors would receive small commemorative Haggadahs as thanks. I still have the tattered, wine-stained, modest booklet that was my favorite. Provided by an orphanage in Jerusalem, with English text opposite the Hebrew, black and white photos of orphans in old-world caps and tiny lace-up boots, photos of the mittel-Europa lady physician who attended them, the booklet also has line drawings, and it was those drawings that provided my enduring image of the transcendent.

"With a mighty hand," the Haggadah recounts, "and with an outstretched arm, God brought us out of Egypt." And there was the drawing, long lines of shuffling slaves in rags, carrying bundles, crossing wasteland, wandering in the desert for 40 years. These were the slaves out of Egypt. Even then I knew who else they were: the remnants of Yiddishkeit, sneaking across borders to the DP camps of post-war Europe. When I see images now of refugees in Africa, Asia, the Middle East, Ukraine, I see that drawing. And I see that mighty hand, that outstretched arm, black lines on white ground, like a streak of lightning, of fire, above their heads. Still that image remains, of the mighty arm and the outstretched hand, the sense of a destiny larger than my personal will or the ego's desire.

*Kitty Hoffman is a writer, spiritual director, and rabbi. Her memoir explores "the resonances between searching for her ancestor, the medieval founder of kabbalah, and growing up among Holocaust survivors." Learn more by visiting Kitty at kittyhoffman.com.*

# Writing as Invitation

*Yes, let the kids read! Let them engage with the stories
and be able to sense themselves as they truly are.*
— Linda Trinh

There's an assumption that religion is behind the surge in book bans, and in some places, that is true. But not all faith practitioners agree with excluding certain stories. For many, spirituality offers a counterpoint to dogmatism and fear-based directives. "Open to Others" speaks to this issue and to values — in this instance, the ethics of helping young readers explore who they are and their place in the world.

## Open to Others by Linda Trinh and Lori Sebastianutti

**Linda**: *What does it feel like to explore who you are?* This was my foundational question while I was writing *The Mystery of the Painted Fan*, the third in The Nguyen Kids early chapter book series, published by Annick Press. Jacob is eight years old and the youngest child in a Vietnamese Canadian family. He begins to question gender stereotypes, explore gender expression and identity, and ponder how these elements intersect with his culture and family expectations.

I felt honored the book was nominated for the 2023 Ontario Library Association's Forest of Reading program Silver Birch Express award. It's humbling to think that more readers may have access to the book.

A month after the nomination, I learned the Waterloo Catholic District School Board (WCDSB) in Ontario had shadow-banned four titles from the Forest of Reading nominated list, including my book baby. Shadow-banning is a term that indicates an internal policy to limit access to a publication.

This incident saddened me and made me wonder — how does spirituality, a theme I write about extensively, relate to the shadow-ban? And more importantly, how does spirituality speak to themes of tolerance and acceptance as a counterpoint to shadow-banning? While the shadow ban at WCDSB has since been lifted, exploring these themes is still a valuable exercise considering the prevalence of book banning happening across Canada and the United States.

**Lori**: After reading *The Mystery of the Painted Fan* with my kids in the spring of 2023, I asked them what they thought.

"Jacob was just trying to be himself," my eight-year-old son answered. My older son and I agreed, and that was the end of the story.

Recently, I reflected on my son's comment and searched for the evidence that supported his main takeaway. Jacob wanted to wear a pink hockey helmet, try nail polish alongside his two older sisters, dance in a cultural festival, and, at the end of the book, be called "Jay" to signify that he wasn't a baby.

The WCDSB had placed Trinh's book in the professional (PRO) section of the library — a section that requires a teacher provide the Catholic context to students (JK-6) before the child is permitted to borrow the book. The Family Life Curriculum guides Ontario's Catholic teachers.

This program aims to help students acquire a Christian vision of personhood, relationships, and sexuality. The curriculum is divided into five strands and organized by grade. When I read about the restrictions, the words that immediately caught my attention were *Catholic context*.

I am a Catholic parent. I was privileged to be educated in Ontario's publicly funded Catholic schools, as was my husband and now our two children. If I had to summarize the "Catholic context" of my 15 years in the system, it would be the emphasis on Jesus's two essential teachings: *Love God and love one another.*

**Linda**: While I was surrounded by Buddhism growing up, I'm now consciously striving to be a spiritual person without the framework of institutional religion. What appeals to me most about faith is the deep connection and love one feels toward other human beings and ultimately, to the universe, to the divine.

I'm compelled to write about how spirituality is interwoven into everyday life. How does faith bump up against other factors of identity such as race and culture? How do all these elements show up in one's self-expression?

Jacob is exploring who he is and his own self-expression. Shadow-banning his story signifies a denial of what it means for young people to develop as full human beings. How is growth and development not aligned with the Family Life Curriculum, at all ages?

**Lori:** Some of the objectives of the Grade 3 Ontario Family Life Curriculum are:

- Students find out more about what it means to be a person … to have feelings and to make choices about the way we express them; and to have talents and gifts that need to be developed.

- Students talk about family names, some family customs, and how family love is open to others, especially when we celebrate special occasions.

- Students discover the importance of learning how to compromise with friends and of being friendly and open to others.

I see no disconnect between Jacob's story and the Family Life Curriculum. Like most eight-year-olds, Jacob knows what it's like to feel misunderstood. Every child wants to be accepted for who they are, and our Catholic faith teaches us that we must accept and love others just as they are.

Halfway through the book, Jacob helps his cousin Hanh make a poster for a club at her school called the GSA. She explains that the club is "where students of all different genders can meet and talk in a safe place." Trinh doesn't clarify for her young readers that GSA stands for Gay-Straight Alliance or Gender-Sexuality Alliance. And what is the Catholic context of mentioning a club that is a safe space for 2SLGBTQIA+ kids?

**Linda**: The same week I found out about the shadow-ban, I received this email from a woman in San Francisco of Vietnamese heritage who had read *The Mystery of the Painted Fan* with her daughter: "My best friend's daughter is transgender and my 6 year old is still processing the change of her 'cousin,' so this book helped us talk about it too. These are the stories I wish I had as a kid, and I'm so thankful my children have it."

As I was feeling very disheartened at the time, I took this message as a sign from the universe that I'm doing what I'm meant to do — tell stories of the challenges and trickiness of childhood. And to tell stories especially for readers whose lived experiences may not currently be represented in books.

While I'm not a practicing Buddhist, I find spiritual meaning in many Buddhist teachings. Vietnamese Buddhist monk Thích Nhất Hạnh spoke of sexual orientation in his book, *Answers From The Heart*. "The spirit of Buddhism is inclusiveness. If you are born gay or lesbian, your ground of being is the same as mine. We are different, but we share the same ground of being. Looking deeply into your nature, you will see yourself as you truly are."

**Lori:** In April of 2023, Pope Francis participated in an 83-minute Spanish-language documentary. He answered questions from ten young people on topics such as sexual identity, feminism, reproductive rights, loss of faith, and more. When asked by a nonbinary youth if there is room for sexual and gender diversity in the Church, Pope Francis replied, "… my duty is always to welcome. The Church cannot close the door to anyone. To no one."

While he upholds traditional church teaching on gender identity, the Pope made his views on the pastoral support of trans people abundantly clear when he said: "For every case, welcome it, accompany it, look into it, discern and integrate it. This is what Jesus would do today."

That's certainly enough Catholic context for me.

**Linda:** I was overjoyed and extremely grateful to learn the shadow-ban had been lifted. Many brave authors, educators, and publishers spoke out, signed petitions and letters, and advocated for all Forest of Reading titles to be available. Yes, let the kids read! Let them engage with the stories and be able to sense themselves as they truly are.

I believe it's valuable for books to be discussed. How does a specific story relate to one's own faith and beliefs? If there are aspects that are challenging or uncomfortable or disruptive, don't hide the book away in the dark. Instead, hold it up to the light, to be examined and questioned. Give the kids more access, not less. Let's talk more, not less.

That is how I envision spirituality in everyday life. Not to be feared and censored. Instead to be discussed, to be relevant, and to embrace empathy and love.

*Linda Trinh is a Vietnamese Canadian author. In addition to The Nguyen Kids early chapter book series with Annick Press, her spiritual memoir will be published by Guernica MiroLand in 2025. Visit Linda at lindaytrinh.com.*

*Lori Sebastianutti's creative nonfiction interrogates infertility, feminism, and the Catholic faith. Essays from her first collection-in-progress appear in award-winning journals and magazines. Learn more when you visit Lori at lorisebastianutti.com.*

# Writing and Resistance

## Tips for Persisting as a Writer by Meharoona Ghani

Currently, I am writing Letters to Rumi: My Journey of Belonging, my spiritual memoir.

A multiple sclerosis diagnosis, challenges with progression, and disability combined with other life experiences such as job loss, the death of a parent, experiences with racism and sexism, etc., led me to Maulana Jalal al-Din Rumi (Rumi), the 13th Century Muslim imam, scholar of Islam and the Qur'an, and I began to write him letters. My book weaves personal stories about overcoming barriers in my quest to find belonging and to retain faith and spirituality in our complex society.

I use poetry as well as prose throughout the letters. This is becoming more common, using hybrid forms — combining poetry and prose, including the use of innovative structures and formats within memoirs to tell stories. I'm thinking of *Persephone's Children* by Rowan McCandless or *Dear Current Occupant* by Chelene Knight.

As marginalized writers, it is important we have supports in place when sharing experiences of spirituality, racism, sexism, etc. I learned this firsthand when excerpts of Letters to Rumi (LTR) appeared in *The Muslimah Who Fell to Earth*, edited by Saima S Hussain and published by Mawenzi House in 2016. A televised show featured the book as part of its book review segment.

Upon reading only two-and-a-half pages of LTR, the host, an imam, singled me out as "anti-religious," [filled with] "resentment for Rumi" and "vulgarities." I was unprepared for this reaction, the amount of energy it took out of me in terms of such uninformed allegations and weighing the question, Do I fight back or not? Was it really about me, or was it his own discomfort? How do I continue to write in the face of such negativity?

My biggest take-away from this experience was self-care centered around patience, calm, persistence, never giving-up, and a community of support. I reached out for support within my network, and one of my contacts wrote to the imam and told him to read the complete excerpt.

He then went back on-air, admitted his mistake, apologized to the viewers, interviewer, to me the author, and to Allah. That was a big deal.

If I could offer advice on coming out as a writer, it would be to ensure you have a core network of mentors, advisors, and supporters. Other tips would be:

1. Sacred practices such as mantras, prayers, meditation, etc., for calm.

2. Hold a reactive response — sometimes it's best not to react immediately, especially if the context of your work is personal. Go into silence, deep listening, sacred space to reflect. Go inward and tap into intuition/heart before you respond.

3. Discernment — think about what's your stuff vs. what's not your stuff.

4. Shut off social media/interactions (for at least two weeks) to remain in a meditative state.

5. Reminders — remind yourself of your vision and purpose in life as a writer.

6. Ask questions — be curious and open.

7. References, references, references!

8. Be responsible and accountable for yourself, your actions, and what you write/say.

9. Choose your battles — not all battles are worth your energy, know your rights regarding security, laws, or human rights legislation in case of extreme situations.

*Meharoona Ghani is a disabled Muslim woman of color, an accomplished writer, educator, and motivational public speaker whose work appears in several prose and poetry collections. Visit Meharoona at mghaniconsulting.ca.*

# Writing and Service

## A New Way Of Publishing by Andi Cumbo & Caroline Topperman

Hi! I'm Andi Cumbo, and I'm Caroline Topperman, and we're the founders of Mountain Ash Press, a hybrid press and publishing services company. We straddle borders and work with an international group of freelancers because we believe that stories are universal.

**Caroline:** As soon as I met Andi, I knew that I wanted to start a business with her, but I didn't know what it should be. The more we spoke about books and the publishing world, the more I realized that our visions aligned. So one day, I suggested we join forces to launch a press where we could help people on their publishing journey. It was very important to me that we honor how our clients wanted to publish their books. I found there was quite a chasm between traditional publishing and self-publishing, and I wanted us to go into this endeavor with open minds.

**Andi:** I immediately said yes to Caroline's offer, and within a month, we had opened Mountain Ash Press. Our mission is to help writers bring their books to the world in the way it feels authentic and meaningful for them. We also hope to fill in some of the gaps that traditional publishing leaves and self-publishing doesn't cover. So far, we've been able to work with a number of talented authors whose work might not otherwise have been published. It's very rewarding work.

**Caroline:** One thing that became clear early on was that we needed to make space for writers whose voices should be heard. So, rather than waiting for people to reach out to us, we make a point of contacting them to offer our help. We are currently working with small groups on an international level to help amplify often silenced voices. We do this on our personal time, then use the press as a vehicle to share their stories on a global scale.

**Andi:** It's also our goal to connect with writers who are local to us. And so, we offer a writers' retreat in Niagara-on-the-Lake, a beautiful historical spot on the river that joins our two countries. This way, we build close relationships with a small group of writers from both countries, and a community of mutual support.

**Caroline:** Another thing that is important to us is that we don't lose touch with our writers, whether we have published them or simply been a part of their journey. We make a point of checking in periodically and asking how we can support them.

**Andi:** Ultimately, we are in this for the writers because we believe that stories matter. As our mission statement says, we believe that storytelling lies at the heart of the human journey, and publishing takes storytelling to a whole new level. We consider it an honor to follow our vocations in this work.

*Andi Cumbo is a Virginia-based writer, Mom, and publisher, and the author of the Stitches In Crime Cozy Mystery Series and the forthcoming Cotswolds Classics series of books.*

*Caroline Topperman is a Toronto-based writer, book coach, and publisher, and the author of the memoir,* Your Roots Cast a Shadow.

*Reach out to Andi and Caroline at info@mountainashpress.*

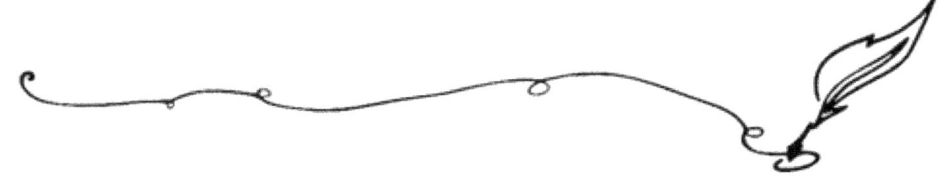

# Chapter 8
# ENDNOTES

*The world is a book and
those who do not travel read only one page.*
— Saint Augustine

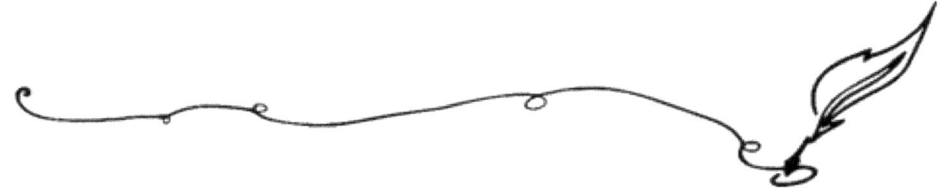

# Resources

*The writer is an explorer. Every step is an advance into a new land.*
— Ralph Waldo Emerson

Build your confidence and your network by building your resources. The QR code below takes you to the Resources page on our online home — spirituallifewriters.com — where you'll find a growing list of recommendations as well as the titles mentioned in the workbook. Ask about these authors at your public library, and order, when you can, from independent bookstores.

Reach out directly to writers whose work you admire and engage with them. And, when the time comes, hand them an autographed copy of your book.

# Acknowledgements

*Alone we can do so little; together we can do so much.*
— Helen Keller

We have saved our acknowledgments for last — a place of honor — because this project would not have been possible without those individuals who nourished, challenged, and accompanied us from the first wild idea to the ultimate completion of *The Spiritual Life Writing Workbook: From Concept to Bookshelf.*

We are grateful for every insightful comment, encouraging word, pointed critique, and sacred reflection offered in the service of writing and publishing this workbook. Special thanks to Steve Sutherland of Creative Connex for pitching this idea and believing we could make it happen. Steve, you never lost sight of our vision, despite the unplanned side trips. Thanks to our beta readers Ron Grimes, Michèle Shannon, and Pat Garrett Taylor, whose responses helped us revise the manuscript with clarity and heart.

We are grateful to Kathy Nutt, our artist and graphic designer, who always responded, "Yes, I can do that," no matter what changes we requested. To Cait Laurenco and the whole team at Creative Connex, and to Kathy, we thank you for your adventurous spirits, charting the course alongside us.

Chapter 7 was inspired by diverse voices featured in *Body & Soul: Stories for Skeptics and Seekers.* In many ways, this workbook builds on that volume, for a whole new audience. Thanks to everyone who graciously agreed to speak up: Andi Cumbo, Adele Dobkowski, Dora Dueck, Hollay Ghadery, Meharoona Ghani, Kitty Hoffman, Sheniz Janmohamed, Pam Johnson, Jónína Kirton, Vickie MacArthur, Lori Sebastianutti, Linda Trinh, Caroline Topperman, and Betsy Warland. You helped sharpen our vision and take our outreach to a whole new level.

And, finally, the driving force behind this workbook is our desire to inspire writers like you, and to welcome you to the world of spiritual life writing. Without you, this workbook would still be a distant dream. Thank you.

# Meet the Authors

Lana Cullis (lanacullis.com) is committed to encouraging kinship among writers. Lana values spiritual life writing as a creative way to access hidden desires, promote healing, and encourage self-determination. She is an ordained lay minister who respects lessons from traditional elders, nature, and family lineage. Lana strives to be a bridge between people of differing faiths. Her writing draws on waking dreams, voices, and visions that reveal the tender places where human truth, individuality, and courage intersect. Lana lives, writes, and plays in qathet, on the West Coast of British Columbia, Canada.

Sharon S. Hines (sharonhines.com) is on a mission to become a better storyteller — and to help others do the same. She writes and teaches with the goal of encouraging spiritual seekers of all stripes to develop a personal relationship with God. She invites writers and readers on a journey to discover the joys, challenges, and hidden benefits of writing down and pondering the stories of their normal, everyday spiritual experiences. She begins from the premise that those who share their spiritual experiences should be acknowledged as truth-tellers, not psychiatric cases. Sharon is a former yankee, now living in Easley, South Carolina.

Susan Scott (susanlscott.ca) is a Great Lakes writer working at the crossroads of story, spirit, self, and culture. She has midwifed dozens of books, including scholarship and memoirs, and has been editing with *The New Quarterly* (TNQ) literary magazine since 2009. Susan has led award-winning initiatives in the environmental humanities and in arts-and-culture work with First Nations, immigrants, and settlers. Edited collections include *Body & Soul: Stories for Skeptics and Seekers*; *Stories in my Neighbour's Faith*; and more. Reach out to Susan for news about groundbreaking work with artists, activists, and adventuresome scholars around the globe.

# Let's Connect

*You can make anything by writing.*
—C.S. Lewis

**As you continue storytelling and writing**, we hope *The Spiritual Life Writing Workbook: From Concept to Bookshelf* will guide you. We know how valuable it is to have companions along the journey. There are several pathways into conversation with us.

Join us at spirituallifewriters.com **to share experiences, questions, or comments** about *The Spiritual Life Writing Workbook: From Concept to Bookshelf.*

**We facilitate custom in-person and online spiritual life writing workshops, retreats, and classes.** We are also interested in other collaborative opportunities. Contact us through our website (spirituallifewriters.com) to find out more. (Or, scan the QR code on this page.)

To reach out to one (or more) of the authors, try these pathways:

**Lana Cullis**
- Website: lanacullis.com
- Email: lanacullis@gmail.com
- Instagram: @writerlanacullis

**Sharon S. Hines**
- Website: sharonhines.com
- Email: sharon@sharonhines.com
- Facebook Page: SharonSHinesAuthor

**Susan Scott**
- Website: susanlscott.ca
- Email: sscott@tnq.ca
- Instagram: @susan_scott_tnq

# Chapter 9
# PROGRESS TRACKER

*It's not about being perfect, it's about being persistent.*
— Anonymous

This at-a-glance log corresponds to all the worksheets.
Use it for accountability,
and to keep track of landmarks you find meaningful or helpful.

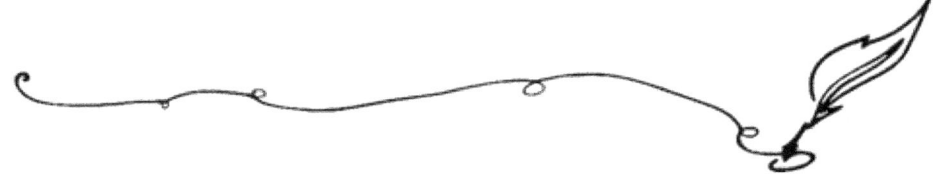

# Introduction

| Worksheet | Milestone | Completed | Notes |
|---|---|---|---|
| 0.1 | Spiritual life writing explored | | |

# Chapter 1 — Let's Get Started

| Worksheet | Milestone | Completed | Notes |
|---|---|---|---|
| 1.1 | Topic chosen | | |
| 1.2 | Story elements spewed & categorized | | |
| 1.3 | Mind map constructed | | |
| 1.4 | Why clarified | | |
| 1.5 | Genre chosen | | |
| 1.6 | Conversation partners identified | | |
| 1.7 | Audience defined | | |
| 1.8 | Personal materials identified | | |
| 1.9 | Relevance and use explored | | |
| 1.10 | Research question(s) framed | | |
| 1.11 | Resources matched to questions | | |

# Chapter 2 — Mapping the Journey

| Worksheet | Milestone | Completed | Notes |
|---|---|---|---|
| 2.1 | Time commitment made | | |
| 2.2 | Story map timeline estimated | | |
| 2.3 | Non-linear story arc defined | | |
| 2.4 | Text-based storyline completed | | |
| 2.5 | Writing style assessed | | |
| 2.6 | Elevator pitch drafted | | |
| 2.7 | Minimal outline drafted | | |
| 2.8 | Outline done | | |

# Chapter 3 — Let's Get Writing

| Worksheet | Milestone | Completed | Notes |
|---|---|---|---|
| 3.1 | Strategy selected for order of writing | | |
| 3.2 | Technology plan in place | | |
| 3.3 | Optional: concerns identified related to chronic conditions | | |
| 3.4 | Optional: tech options explored to minimize chronic limitations | | |
| 3.5 | World-building and voice explored | | |
| 3.6 | Spiritual vocabulary established | | |
| 3.7 | Writing into the Sacred exercises tried or completed | | |
| 3.8 | Diverse feedback solicited | | |
| | Junk draft completed | | |
| | Structure draft completed | | |
| | Rough draft completed | | |
| | Surgery draft completed | | |
| | Last draft completed | | |

# Chapter 4 — Editing and Polishing

| Worksheet | Milestone | Completed | Notes |
|---|---|---|---|
| 4.1 | Questions for editor(s) drafted | | |
| 4.2 | Contemplative practice completed | | |
| 4.3 | Revising and self-editing planned | | |
| 4.4 | Supportive rituals developed | | |
| 4.5 | Permissions tracked | | |
| 4.6 | Permission materials customized | | |
| | Polished manuscript completed | | |

# Chapter 5 — Publishing and Promotion

| Worksheet | Milestone | Completed | Notes |
|:---:|---|---|---|
| 5.1 | Existing author platform assessed | | |
| 5.2 | Publishing preferences identified | | |
| 5.3 | Community connections explored | | |
| 5.4 | Newsletter topics considered | | |
| 5.5 | Author website designed or built | | |
| 5.6 | Domain name registered | | |
| 5.7 | Online activity established | | |

# Chapter 6 — Reflecting, Celebrating, and Beyond

| Worksheet | Milestone | Completed | Notes |
|---|---|---|---|
| 6.1 | Processes reviewed and debriefed | | |
| 6.2 | Journey noticed | | |
| 6.3 | "Why" celebrate identified | | |
| 6.4 | Celebration planned | | |
| 6.5 | Energizing creative activities identified | | |
| 6.6 | Creativity resources consulted | | |

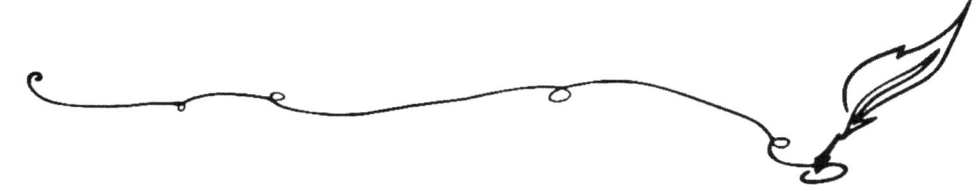